Spectacular Friends!

A Step-by-Step Guide to 34 Sensational Designs

Ariela Pshednovek

Photography by Ran Lurie

imagine!

An Imagine Book
Published by Charlesbridge
85 Main Street, Watertown, MA 02472
617-926-0329
www.charlesbridge.com

Created by Penn Publishing Ltd.

Editor-in-Chief: Rachel Penn
Edited by Shoshana Brickman
Photography by Ran Lurie
Styling by Oranit Wasserman
Make up by Natalie Arnautoff
Design and layout by Ariane Rybski

Library of Congress Cataloging-in-Publication Data

Pshednovek, Ariela.
 Spectacular friendship bracelets : a step-by-step guide to 34 sensational
designs / Ariela Pshednovek ; photography by Ran Lurie.
    pages cm
 "An Imagine book"—Title page verso.
 ISBN 978-1-62354-081-4 (softcover)
 ISBN 978-1-60734-961-7 (ebook)
 ISBN 978-1-60734-962-4 (ebook pdf)
 1. Jewelry making. 2. Friendship bracelets. I. Title.

 TT212.P75 2016
 745.594'2--dc23   2015007588

10 9 8 7 6 5 4 3 2 1

Contents

Designs

Introduction

Friendship is such an important part of life—and friendship bracelets are a terrific way of celebrating it. Even in today's technological world, with all the devices and gadgets that surround us every day, there is something wonderfully authentic about friendship bracelets. They are a meaningful way of showing you care (without spending tons of money). They are a token of love, friendship and gratitude, and are also easy to make!

Friendship bracelets are often made with a specific person in mind; this makes them imminently more meaningful than any store-bought trinket. Plus, friendship bracelets are the perfect size for tucking into an envelope to mail, slipping into a schoolbag as a surprise gift, or decorating a larger gift.

Spectacular Friendship Bracelets is a colorful collection of more than 30 friendship bracelets. Some of the bracelet designs are elegant and sophisticated; others are playful and fun. Some designs call for patience and careful knotting; others just require applying glue and adding colorful findings. There is something for everyone, and every design can be adapted to the colors you love or available materials.

Each design in *Spectacular Friendship Bracelets* comes with an estimation of how long it will take to make (none take more than 1 hour!), is ranked according to difficulty, and accompanied by step-by-step full-color photographs. The size of many designs is adjustable, which is an advantage if you're making the bracelet for a surprise gift, as it doesn't need to be measured in advance.

Before you start, make sure you have all the necessary tools and materials. If you need scissors, make sure they are sharp; if you need a lighter, make sure it works. If you're using beads or buttons, make sure they fit on your string or cord. Don't feel bound by the materials and colors described in the book; choose the materials you love, and enjoy the process of creating with them.

About the Author

Ariela Pshednovek is an artist and jewelry designer who specializes in creating unique pieces of jewelry that combine energy, color and light. Ariela has a passion for diverse textures and materials, and draws inspiration from the natural world to create jewelry that is strong, special and distinct. Ariela's jewelry is sold in fine shops worldwide, and has been featured in dozens of photo shoots in leading fashion magazines.

Tools

You don't need a toolbox the size of a toaster oven to make these fabulous designs. Many of them can be made with just scissors and a needle! Here's a complete list of the tools used for these projects:

Leather hole punch - This is used to make holes in leather wristbands. Most leather hole punches come with several sizes of holes to suit even the thinnest bands. (Fig. A)

Lighter - This is used to melt the ends of the cords. Make sure you have adult supervision when using a lighter.

Needle - This is used for sewing on chains and for stringing beads. If you're using it for the latter, make sure the eye of your needle is thick enough to string your thread, but not so thick that it can't fit through the bead holes.

Pliers - These are used to open and close jump rings, crimp end caps, and press down stud prongs. In some cases, you can use a pair of sturdy scissors instead (for example, to press down stud prongs), but don't try to cut wire or chains with scissors, as it often just bends the chain and/or dulls the scissors. (Fig. B)

Scissors - You'll need a pair of sturdy scissors that can cut waxed cord, nylon cords and embroidery floss. Make sure you keep your scissors close to your other beading supplies so that you don't have to look for them every time you want to cut a thread! (Fig. C)

A

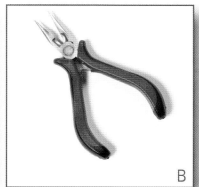

B

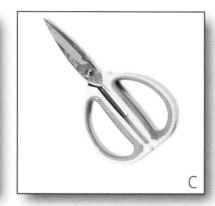

C

Materials

The materials used in these projects are easy to find at craft stores and online. In all projects, you can replace the materials I've used with ones of your own choosing. Just make sure that all the materials can be strung as required (you don't want beads with holes that are too small for your waxed cord, for example), and make sure you have all of the materials you'll be using on hand before you start.

Beads - I've specified the size and color of all the beads used in these designs, but you can certainly adjust according to your own style, or according to what's readily available to you. Most bead measurements are given in millimeters, as this is how they are often sold, but you can certainly use similar beads that aren't the same dimensions if they look right and fit. As for the seed beads, these are measured with a /0 numbering system. The number refers to the number of beads, per inch, when laid flat. The smaller the number, the larger the bead (so 11/0 is smaller than 8/0).

Buttons – These are used for closing bracelets and as a decorative embellishment.

Charms – A variety of charms, made from various metals as well as other materials, are used in these projects.

Embroidered bands – These bands add a colorful element to several leather wristbands. They can be found online and in shops that sell sewing notions. A box of old sewing odds and ends can serve as a treasure chest of embroidered bands.

Embroidery floss – This soft cotton thread comes in a wide variety of colors. Each piece is actually made of six thin strands of thread.

Findings – Gold and silver jump rings, clasps and cord ends are used in some designs to close the bracelets, or to add decorative accents. Make sure the findings you choose are of good quality and the right size for the other materials in your bracelet.

Glue – This is used to affix knots at the end of bracelets, affix embellishments, etc. I recommend using E6000 glue for most projects. Long lasting and durable, it dries clear and is resistant to water.

Knotted bracelets – These can be handmade, of course, but they can also be purchased readymade online or at craft stores. They come in a wide variety of colors, styles and lengths.

Leather wristbands – Soft leather wristbands are used as a base for several of the bracelets in this book. They come in various widths and lengths, and often have two snaps, which makes them adjustable.

Leather cord – This flexible cord comes in various diameters and colors. If you want to affix cord ends at each end of the cord, make sure you buy ones that are the right size for the selected cord.

Metal, rhinestone and rock chains – These are used as sparkly accessories in several bracelets. Chains can be purchased online or in embellishment shops. If you purchase chains that are longer than you need for a specific project, make sure you have wire cutters on hand to cut them.

Rhinestone and studs – These shiny embellishments can be added to bracelets with ease. Some of them come with prongs that can be folded over and screwed in; others have a flat back that just needs to be glued in place.

Tape – This is used in several designs to hold the bracelet in place on a tabletop as you work.

Waxed cord – This is an excellent type of cord for friendship bracelets of all sorts, as it is smooth, durable and doesn't fray over time. Waxed cord is perfect for knotting and allows for a smooth finish, as the ends melt beautifully. Waxed cord comes in a wide variety of colors. The standard diameter of waxed cord is 1.0 mm, but it also comes in 0.8 mm diameter, which is what you'll need for stringing beads with very small holes.

Techniques

The techniques used in these bracelets are really quite simple, and once you practice a few times, I'm sure you'll get the hang of it. Here's a short summary of what you'll need to know:

Overhand knot

This knot can be used to secure beads in place, start bracelets, and finish them. It is also a knot you probably use every day to tie your shoes! Here's how it works:

1. Make a loop in the cord.

2. Insert one end of the cord (doesn't matter which) in the loop.

3. Pull this end through the loop to finish.

Lark's head knot

This type of knot is used to affix cord to other objects (such as other pieces of cord, loops, hoops, or jump rings).

1. Fold the cord in half.

2. Place the looped part of the cord under the other object (cord, loop, hoop, or jump ring).

3. Draw the trails of the looped cord over the object (cord, loop, hoop or jump ring) and through the loop in the cord.

4. Pull to secure and finish.

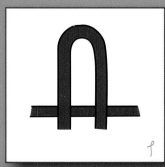 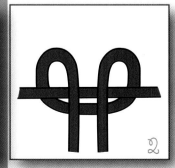 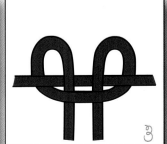 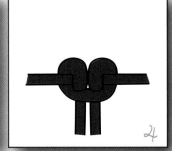

Square knot

This knot, also known as a flat knot or reef knot, is a basic knot for many macramé designs. It requires a minimum of three cords – two tying cords and one base cord – but it is often made with four cords, in which case there are two base cords and two tying cords. Keep the base cords taut as you work, to ensure that the knots come out flat.

1. Attach the cords in the correct order. Bring the left cord over the center cords and under the right cord. Bring the right cord over the left cord and under the center cords.

2. Draw the right cord up through the loop between the left cord and the center cords.

3. Pull the right cord and left cords firmly to tighten.

4. Bring the cord on the right over the center cords.

5. Bring the cord on the left over the cord from the right and under the center cords.

6. Bring the cord from the left over the cord from the right.

7. Pull the right cord and left cords firmly to tighten.

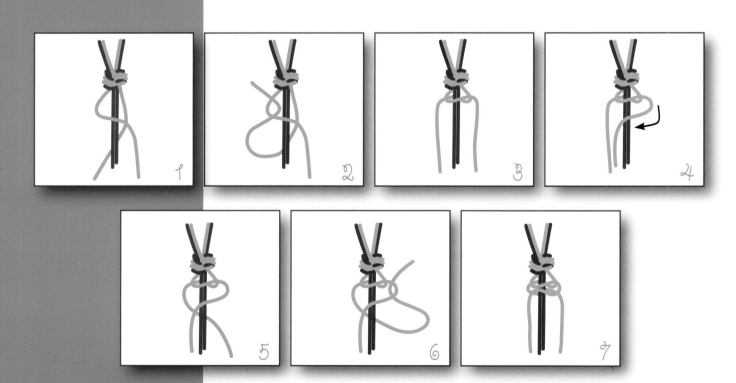

Beaded square knot

This knot is based on the square knot, but includes the addition of beads. You can either string the beads on the base cords (these are the cords that don't move) or onto the tying cords (these are the cords on the left and right sides).

1. Attach the cords in the correct order. Bring the left cord over the center cords and under the right cord. Bring the right cord over the left cord and under the center cords.

2. Draw the right cord up through the loop between the left cord and the center cords.

3. Pull the right cord and left cords firmly to tighten.

4. String a bead on the center cords and then bring the cord on the right over the center cords, just below the bead.

5. Bring the cord on the left over the cord from the right and under the center cords, just below the bead.

6. Bring the cord from the left over the cord from the right.

7. Pull the right cord and left cords firmly to tighten them flush against the bead.

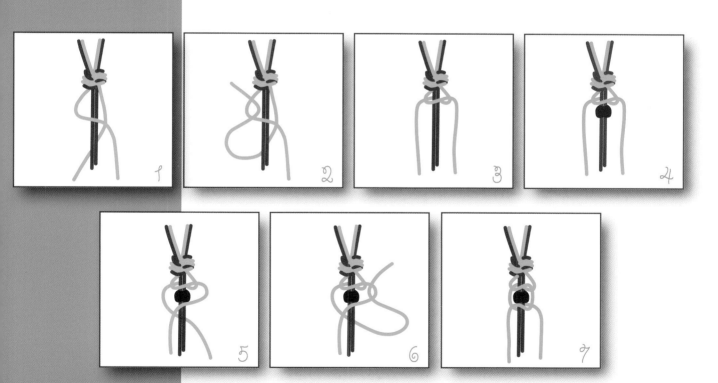

French knot

This knot, also known as a half knot or spiral knot, looks more intricate than the square knot, but it's actually one step easier. Rather than alternating between which cord starts each knot, these knots all start with the same cord.

1. Attach the cords in the correct order. Bring the left cord over the center cords and under the right cord. Bring the right cord under the center cords and over the left cord.

2. Bring the right cord up through the loop between the center cords and the left cord.

3. Pull the cords to tighten.

4. Repeat this process, always starting with the same cord.

5. Pull the right cord and left cords firmly after each knot to tighten the knots.

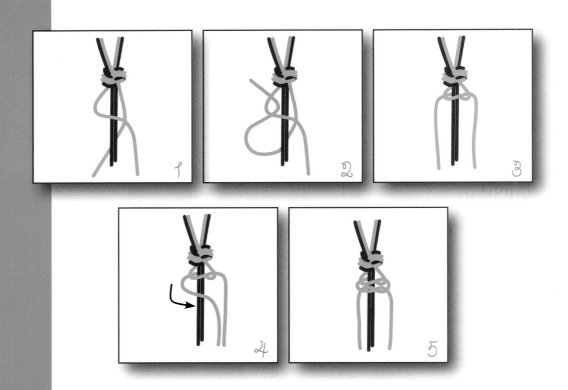

Overcast stitch

This common stitch, also known as a whipstitch, is an easy way of sewing two pieces of fabric together. In these bracelets, it is also used to secure chains onto wristbands.

1. Thread a needle with thread and tie a knot at one end of the thread. Insert the needle into the backside of the fabric and draw it up through the front.

2. Wrap the thread around the object you want to affix and then insert the needle back down into the fabric.

3. Insert the needle again into the backside of the fabric, not far from where it came out, and draw up it through the front of the fabric.

4. Repeat steps 2 and 3 until you have secured the object onto the fabric.

5. Tie a double knot in the thread on the backside of the fabric and trim the ends to about ¼".

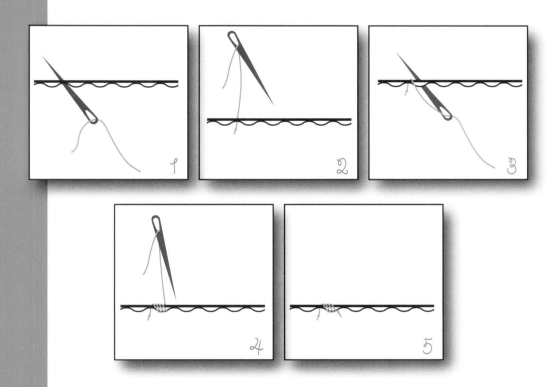

Awesome Onyx Bracelet

Just because it's got glitter doesn't mean this bracelet is hard to make. In fact, it's actually really easy. Just use a glittery ball for the centerpiece and you've got a fabulous, fun bracelet in minutes!

Materials & Tools
(Fig. A)
- **Red waxed cord**
- **24 round faceted black and white beads, 6 mm**
- **1 disco ball bead, 8 mm**
- **Scissors**
- **Lighter**

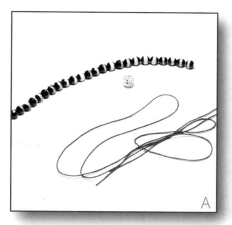

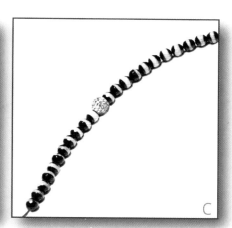

1. Cut a 16" piece of red waxed cord. String on 11 black and white beads and 1 disco ball bead. (Fig. B)

2. String on the other 11 black and white beads. (Fig. C)

3. Tie knots at both ends of the bracelet to secure the beads in place. Make sure the knots are flush against the beads, and allow for a 2" tail after each knot. Cut an 8" piece of waxed cord. Wrap the tails of the bracelet over each other in opposite directions, and place the 8" piece of cord under them. Tie the cord in a square knot over the tails of the bracelet, holding them in place.

4. Tie 4 more square knots in the 8" piece of cord, making a closure for the bracelet. Trim the cord about ¼" from the last square knot and melt the ends. (Fig. D)

5. String 1 black and white bead on each bracelet tail. (Fig. E)

6. Tie a knot after each bead, about 1½" from the closure. Trim the cord about ¼" from the knot and then melt the ends. (Fig. F)

Bright and Bold Bracelet

This bracelet follows a simple pattern that can be recreated with any collection of beads that you like. Choose a charm that suits the friend who is on the receiving end.

Materials & Tools
(Fig. A)

- **Black waxed cord**
- **14 round faceted turquoise beads, 6 mm**
- **18 round faceted coral beads, 6 mm**
- **6 round black onyx beads, 8 mm**
- **1 gold and rhinestone rondelle, with hoop**
- **1 gold heart charm**
- Scissors
- Pliers
- Lighter

15
minutes

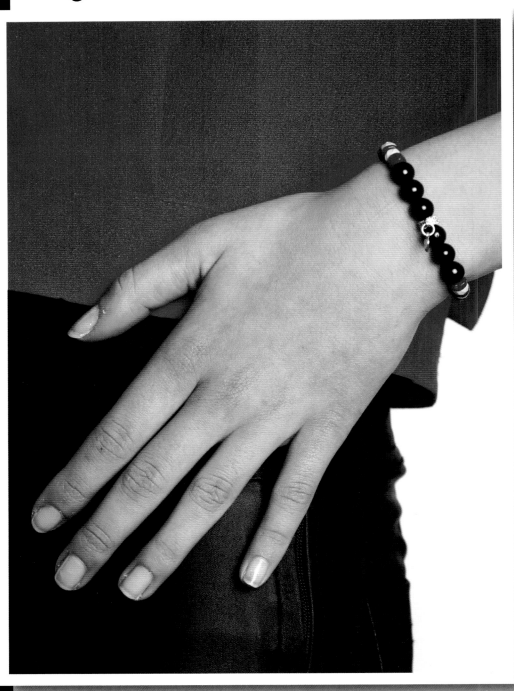

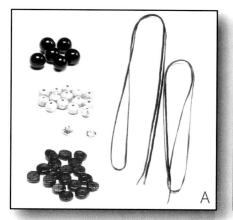

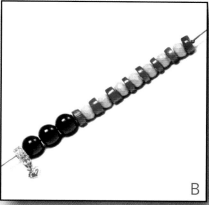

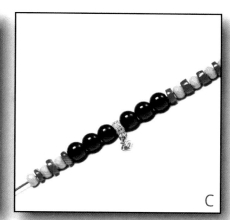

1. Cut a 16" piece of black waxed cord, and string on 1 coral bead and 1 turquoise bead. String on 7 more coral beads alternating with 6 more turquoise beads, then string on 3 black onyx beads and the 1 gold and rhinestone rondelle. Using pliers, open the hoop on the rondelle. String on the heart charm and close the loop. (Fig. B)

2. String on 3 black onyx beads, and then 3 coral bead alternating with 3 turquoise beads. (Fig. C)

3. String on 5 more coral beads alternating with 4 turquoise beads. End with a coral bead. Move the beads to the middle of the cord and tie knots at either end to secure them in place.

4. Cut an 8" piece of black waxed cord. Wrap the tails of the bracelet over each other in opposite directions and place the 8" piece of cord under them. Tie this cord in a square knot over the tails of the bracelet, holding them in place. (Fig. D)

5. Tie 4 more square knots in the 8" piece of cord, making a closure for the bracelet. Trim the cord about ¼" from the last square knot and melt the ends. String 1 coral bead on each bracelet tail and then make a knot after each bead, about 1½" from the closure. (Fig. E)

6. Trim the cord about ¼" from the last square knot and then melt the ends. (Fig. F)

Turquoise and Red Bracelet

The waxed cord in this bracelet is very prominent, as it is used to tie a beadlike knot between each bead. Make sure you use a needle to draw the knots flush against the beads.

Materials & Tools
(Fig. A)

- **Red waxed cord**
- **28 round faceted turquoise beads, 6 mm**
- **1 red, turquoise and gold Tibetan bead, 2 cm**
- **Scissors**
- **Needle**
- **Lighter**

 20 minutes

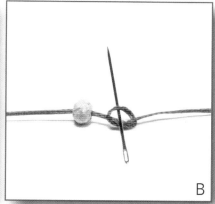

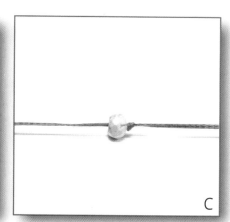

A

B

C

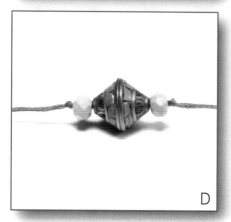

D

E

F

1. Cut a 24" piece of red waxed cord and string on 1 turquoise bead. Draw it to the middle of the cord. Tie a loose knot in the cord, near the turquoise beads that you just strung. Insert a needle into the knot and use the needle to draw the knot until it is flush with the turquoise bead. (Fig. B) Remove the needle and pull the knot tight to secure it. (Fig. C)

2. String the Tibetan bead onto the cord and draw it up to the turquoise bead (not the knot). String on another turquoise bead and draw it up until it is flush with the Tibetan bead. Make a loose knot in the cord and draw it up using a needle until it is flush with the turquoise bead. Remove the needle and pull the knot tight to secure. (Fig. D)

3. Continuing stringing turquoise beads onto each side of the bracelet, one bead at a time, and drawing each bead up until it is flush with the knot. Then make a knot in the cord adjacent to the bead and draw it flush with the bead using a needle.

4. Repeat this process to string a total of 13 turquoise beads on each side of the bracelet. Cut a 10" piece of waxed cord. Wrap the tails of the bracelet over each other in opposite directions and place the 10" piece of cord under them. Tie this cord in a square knot over the tails of the bracelet, holding them in place.

5. Tie another 7 square knots in the 10" piece of cord, securing the ends of the bracelet in place and making a closure for the bracelet. Trim the cord about ¼" from the last square knot and then melt the ends. (Fig. E)

6. String a turquoise bead on each bracelet tail and then make a knot about 1½" from the closure. Trim the cord about ¼" from the knot and then melt the ends. (Fig. F)

Charmer's Charm Bracelet

This bracelet will bring you good luck whenever you wear it. I've described the color pattern in this design, but you can choose your own favorite colors and patterns.

Materials & Tools
(Fig. A)

- Black waxed cord
- 4 flat oval faceted orange beads, 4 mm
- 8 flat oval faceted burgundy beads, 4 mm
- 12 round faceted yellow beads, 4 mm
- 8 flat oval faceted black beads, 4 mm
- 8 flat oval faceted turquoise beads, 4 mm
- 6 round faceted black and white beads, 6 mm
- 1 silver charm
- Scissors
- Lighter

15
minutes

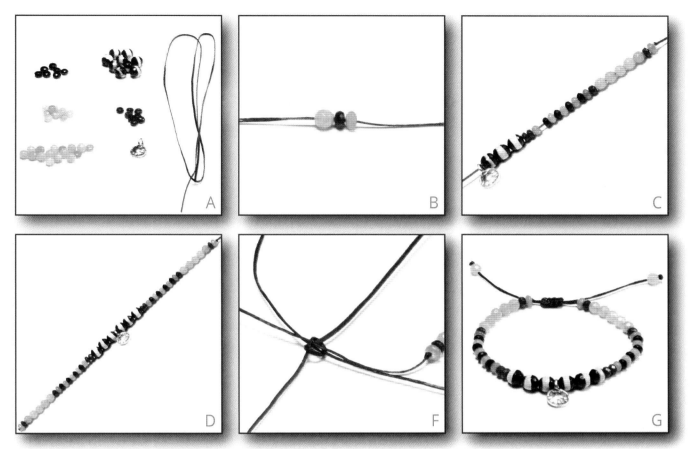

1. Cut a 16" piece of black waxed cord. Tie a knot at one end of the cord, leaving a 2" tail. String on 1 orange bead, 1 burgundy bead and 1 yellow bead. (Fig. B)

2. String on the rest of the beads on this side of the bracelet in the following order: 4 yellow beads, 1 burgundy bead and 1 orange bead. Now string on 4 black beads alternating with 4 turquoise beads, then string on 2 burgundy beads. String on 3 black and white beads and then string on the silver charm. (Fig. C)

3. Now repeat the pattern in reverse on the other side of the silver charm. First string on 3 black and white beads, then 2 burgundy beads, and then 1 turquoise bead and 1 black bead. Now string on 3 more turquoise beads alternating with 3 more black beads. String on 1 orange bead, 1 burgundy bead, 5 yellow beads, 1 burgundy and 1 yellow bead. (Fig. D)

4. Cut an 8" piece of waxed cord. Wrap the tails of the bracelet over each other in opposite directions and place the 8" piece of cord under them. Tie this cord in a square knot over the tails of the bracelet, holding them in place. Tie another 4 square knots in the 8" piece of cord, making a closure for the bracelet. Trim the cord about ¼" from the last square knot and then melt the ends. (Fig. E)

5. String 1 yellow bead on each bracelet tail. Make a knot after each bead, about 1½" from the closure. Trim each cord about ¼" from the knot and melt the end. (Fig. F)

Elegant Eternity Bracelet

This elegant design has just the right amount of glitter. You can choose any shape for the center charm, but I find that the eternity symbol is ideal.

Materials & Tools
(Fig. A)

- **Black waxed cord**
- **1 rhinestone and gold infinity charm, with loops**
- **5 round twisted corrugated gold beads, 2 mm**
- **38 flat oval faceted black onyx beads, 4 mm**
- **Scissors**
- **Lighter**

15 minutes

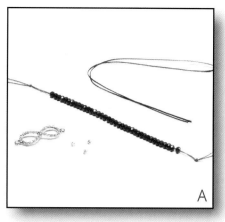

A

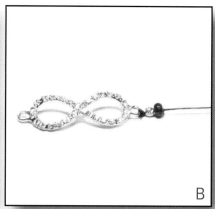

B

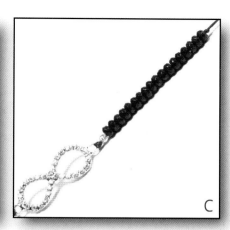

C

D

E

F

1. Cut a 10" piece of black waxed cord. String one end of the cord through one of the loops of the infinity charm and tie an overhand knot to secure it. Trim the tail of the knot to ¼" and melt the end. String on 1 corrugated gold bead and 1 black onyx bead. (Fig. B)

2. String on another 17 black onyx beads and then tie a secure knot after the last bead. Make sure the knot is flush against the bead so that the beads don't move on the cord. (Fig. C)

3. Cut another 10" piece of waxed cord, secure it to the other loop in the charm with an overhand knot. String on 1 corrugated gold bead and then 18 black onyx beads onto the cord.

4. Tie a knot after the last bead. String 1 corrugated gold bead onto one bracelet tail. String the other tail through the same bead, but in the opposite direction. (Fig. D)

5. Cut an 8" piece of waxed cord and put it under the tails of the bracelet. (The tails will already be in opposite directions, because of the bead you strung previously.) Tie the cord in a square knot over the tails of the bracelet, on one side of the bead. (Fig. E)

6. Tie another 3 square knots on this side of the bead, then bring the cords to the other side of the bead and tie 3 more square knots. Trim the ends of the cord about ¼" from the last square knot and melt the ends.

7. String 1 corrugated gold bead and 1 black onyx bead on each bracelet tail. Make a knot about 1½" from the end of each tail. Trim the cord about ¼" from the knot and then melt the ends. (Fig. F)

Rosy Rainbow Tassel Bracelet

This playful design features the lovely juxtaposition of a rainbow fringe and a golden skeleton.

Materials & Tools
(Fig. A)

Fuchsia waxed cord

9 pieces of embroidery floss, various colors, 3" each

1 gold skull bead, with vertical hole

20 round faceted rose quartz beads, 8 mm

1 round smooth gold bead, 4 mm

2 flat oval faceted rose quartz beads, 6 mm

Scissors

Lighter

 20 minutes

22

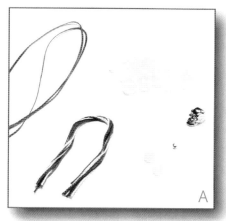

A

B

C

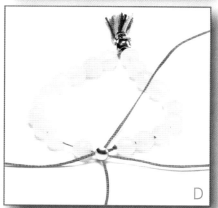

D

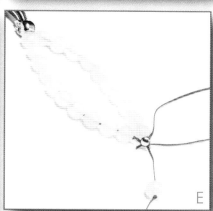

E

F

1. Cut a 20" piece of fuchsia waxed cord. Gather the pieces of embroidery floss together and place them in the middle of the waxed cord. Tie the cord around the embroidery floss in a double knot. Trim the ends of the floss so that all 18 ends are even. String both ends of the waxed cord through the hole in the gold skull bead and draw the bead down to the knot holding the floss to make a tassel. (Fig. B)

2. Separate the two waxed cords and string 10 round rose quartz beads onto one of the cords. (Fig. C) Tie a knot that is flush with the last bead to secure the beads in place.

3. Repeat this process on the other cord, stringing 10 round rose quartz beads onto the cord and then tying a knot that is flush with the last bead. String 1 round smooth gold bead onto one bracelet tail.

4. String the other tail through the same bead, but in the opposite direction. Cut an 8" piece of waxed cord and place it under the tails of the bracelet. (The tails will already be in opposite directions, because of the bead you strung previously.) (Fig. D)

5. Tie 4 square knots over the tails of the bracelet, on one side of the gold bead. Draw both sides of the cord to the other side of the gold bead, and tie 4 more knots. Cut the ends of the cord about ¼" from the last square knot and melt the ends. String a flat oval rose quartz bead on each bracelet tail. (Fig. E)

6. Make a knot about 1½" from the end of each tail. Trim the cord about ¼" from the knot and then melt the ends. (Fig. F)

Ivory Elegance Tassel Bracelet

This elegant design features a soft white fringe and beautiful ivory beads. Interspersing gold rondelle beads adds a simple touch of elegance.

Materials & Tools
(Fig. A)

- Cream waxed cord
- 20 round cream ivory beads, 8 mm
- 4 gold daisy rondelles, 2 mm
- 1 ivory fringe
- Scissors
- Lighter

15 minutes

A

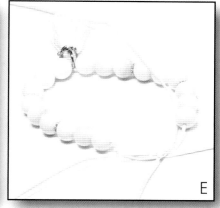

B

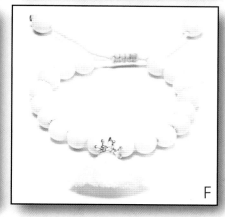

C

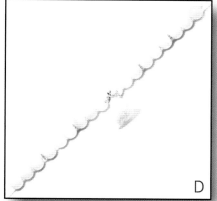

D

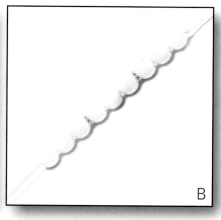

E

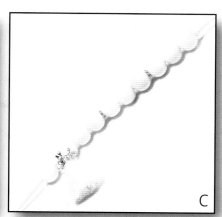

F

1. Cut a 16" piece of cream waxed cord, and string on 3 ivory beads, 1 gold daisy rondelle, 3 ivory beads, 1 gold daisy rondelle, and 3 ivory beads. Tie a knot on one side of the beads, leaving a 4" tail. (Fig. B)

2. String on the ivory fringe and then string on 1 ivory bead. (Fig. C)

3. String on 2 ivory beads, 1 gold daisy rondelle, 3 ivory beads, 1 gold daisy rondelle, and 3 ivory beads. (Fig. D)

4. Tie a knot at this end of the bracelet, securing the beads in place. Cut an 8" piece of waxed cord. Wrap the tails of the bracelet over each other in opposite directions and place the 8" piece of cord under them.

5. Tie this cord in a square knot over the tails of the bracelet, holding them in place. (Fig. E)

6. Tie another 4 square knots in the 8" piece of cord, making a closure for the bracelet. Trim the cord about ¼" from the last square knot and then melt the ends.

7. String 1 ivory bead on each bracelet tail. Make a knot after each bead, about 1½" from the closure. Trim the cord about ¼" from the knot and then melt the ends. (Fig. F)

Glittery Burgundy Bracelet

This divine bracelet combines semi-precious stone beads with round twisted corrugated gold beads for great elegance.

Materials & Tools
(Fig. A)

Black waxed cord

50 flat oval faceted burgundy beads, 4 mm

15 round twisted corrugated gold beads, 2 mm

Scissors

Lighter

20
minutes

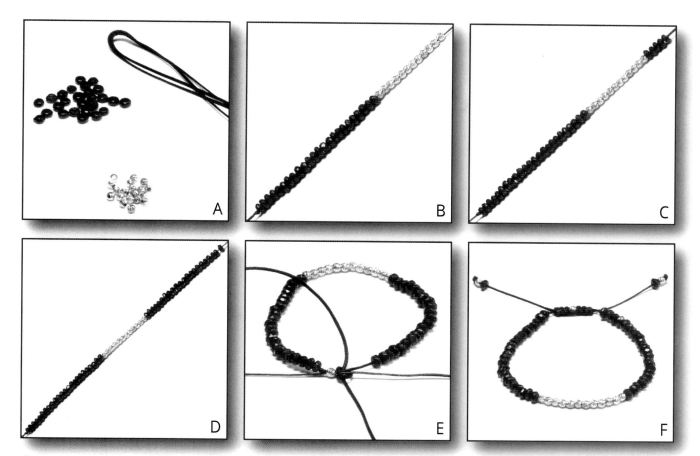

A

B

C

D

E

F

1. Cut a 16" piece of black waxed cord, and tie a knot a one end, leaving a 2" tail. String on 24 burgundy beads and then string on 12 corrugated gold beads. (Fig. B)

2. String on 5 more burgundy beads. (Fig. C)

3. String on 19 more burgundy beads. (Fig. D)

4. Tie a knot at this end of the bracelet, flush with the last bead. String 1 corrugated gold bead onto one bracelet tail. String the other bracelet tail through the same bead, but in the opposite direction. (Fig. E)

5. Cut an 8" piece of waxed cord and put it under the tails of the bracelet. (The tails will already be in opposite directions, because of the bead you strung previously.) Tie 4 square knots in the 8" piece of cord on one side of the gold bead, and then bring the cords to the other side of the bead and tie 4 more square knots.

6. Trim the cord about ¼" from the last square knot and then melt the ends. String 1 burgundy bead and 1 corrugated gold bead on each bracelet tail.

7. Make a knot about 1½" from the end of each tail. Trim the cord about ¼" from the knot and then melt the ends. (Fig. F)

Infinite Energy Bracelet

This colorful bracelet has an infinite amount of positive energy. The turquoise and yellow waxed cords have a lovely delicate effect on the transparent faceted beads.

Materials & Tools
(Fig. A)

- Yellow waxed cord
- 1 gold infinity charm
- Tape
- Turquoise waxed cord
- 14 round faceted transparent beads, 8 mm
- 2 round textured gold beads, 8 mm
- Scissors
- Lighter

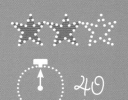

40 minutes

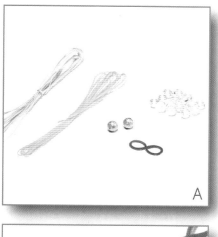

A

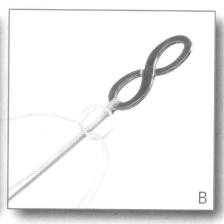

B

C

D

E

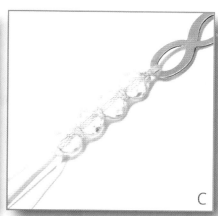

F

1. Cut a 20" piece of yellow waxed cord. Fold it in half and attach it to one end of the infinity charm using a lark's head knot. These will be the base cords for this half of the bracelet. Tape the infinity charm to a tabletop to hold it in place. Cut a 25" piece of turquoise waxed cord and place the middle of it just below the lark's head knot. Make sure the ends of the turquoise cord extend evenly on either side of the base cords. These will be the tying cords. Tie 2 square knots in the turquoise tying cords, anchoring them to the yellow base cords. Draw the knots so they are flush with the infinity charm. (Fig. B)

2. String 1 transparent bead onto the base cords and draw it up to the knots. Bring the tying cords around the bead and tie them in 2 square knots after the bead, securing it in place. Repeat this process to secure 3 more beads onto the base cords. Secure each bead with 2 square knots tied using the turquoise tying cords. (Fig. C)

3. Repeat this process to secure 3 more beads onto the base cords in this manner. (Fig. D)

4. When 7 transparent beads have been strung, tie a double knot using the turquoise tying cords immediately after the last bead. Trim the turquoise cords about ¼" from the knot and melt the ends. String 1 textured gold bead onto the yellow cord, and make a knot about 2" from the last knot in the turquoise cords. Trim the yellow cord to about ¼" from the knot, and melt the ends. (Fig. E)

5. Cut another 20" piece of yellow waxed cord, fold it in half, and secure it to the to the other side of the infinity charm with a lark's head knot. Repeat the process of stringing beads and tying knots on the other side of the bracelet.

6. Cut an 8" piece of yellow waxed cord. Wrap the tails of the bracelet over each other in opposite directions and place the 8" piece of cord under them. Tie the cord in a square knot over the tails of the bracelet, holding them in place. Tie another 4 square knots in the 8" piece of cord, making a closure for the bracelet. Trim the ends of the cord about ¼" from the last square knot and then melt the ends. (Fig. F)

Lucky Ladder Bracelet

This knotted bracelet, which features turquoise beads in a ladder-like pattern on both sides of a central charm, is sure to bring good luck to any look. Make sure that the holes in your beads are large enough to allow the waxed cord to slide in easily.

Materials & Tools
(Fig. A)

- Red waxed cord
- 1 gold octagon charm, with loops
- Tape
- 44 turquoise seed beads, 8/0
- Scissors
- Lighter

45 minutes

A

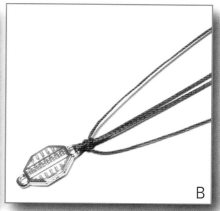

B

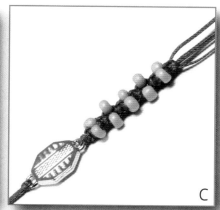

C

D

E

F

1. Cut a 10" piece of red waxed cord. Fold it in half and attach it to one of the loops in the octagon charm with a lark's head knot. These will be the base cords for this half of the bracelet. Tape the octagon charm to a tabletop to hold it in place. Cut a 35" piece of waxed cord and place the middle of it just below the lark's head knot. Make sure the cord extends evenly on either side of the base cord. These will be the tying cords, and they'll also be the cords onto which you string the beads.

2. Tie 2 square knots in the tying cords, anchoring them to the base cords. Draw the knots so they are flush with the octagon charm. (Fig. B) String 1 turquoise seed bead onto each tying cord, and then tie 3 square knots over the base cords, securing the beads in place.

3. Repeat this process another 4 times, stringing pairs of turquoise beads onto the tying cords and then securing these cords to the base cords with 3 square knots. (Fig. C)

4. Repeat this process to string a total of 10 pairs of beads onto this side of the octagon charm. End with 3 square knots, and then trim the cords about ¼" from the knot and melt the ends.

5. Repeat this entire process on the other side of the charm, cutting 10" and 35" inch pieces of red cord and then stringing on 20 turquoise seed beads.

6. Cut an 8" piece of waxed cord. Wrap the tails of the bracelet (there will be two on each side) over each other in opposite directions and place the 8"

piece of cord under them. Tie the cord in a square knot over the tails of the bracelet, holding them in place. (Fig. D)

7. Tie another 4 square knots in the 8" piece of cord, making a closure for the bracelet. Trim the ends of the cord about ¼" from the last square knot and melt the ends. On one side of the bracelet, string 1 turquoise bead on each bracelet tail. Make a knot after each bead about 2" from the last square knot, and then melt the ends. (Fig. E)

8. Repeat this process on the other side of the bracelet, stringing 1 turquoise bead on each bracelet tail, making a knot after each bead about 2" from the last square knot, and then melting the ends. (Fig. F)

Golden Tube Bracelet

This design features gold tube beads that line up horizontally rather than end-to-end, and diamond buttons for the centerpiece and clasp. The bracelet size can't be adjusted, so check the length of the bracelet before stringing on the centerpiece button and add (or subtract) beads as required.

Materials & Tools
(Fig. A)

- **Purple waxed cord**
- **Tape**
- **32 gold tube beads, 7 mm**
- **1 rhinestone and gold button, 6 mm**
- **1 rhinestone and gold button, 8 mm**
- **Glue**
- **Scissors**
- **Lighter**

30 *minutes*

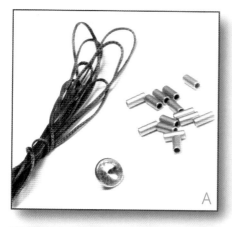

A

B

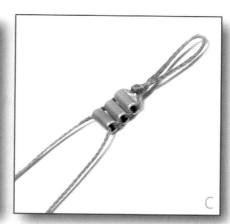

C

D

E

F

1. Cut a 5" piece of purple waxed cord, fold it in half, and tie an overhand knot at the folded end to form a loop. Make sure the loop is large enough to slip over the larger rhinestone and gold button. Tape the loop to a tabletop to hold it in place. String 1 gold tube bead onto one of the cords, and draw it up towards the loop.

2. Now draw the other cord through the same bead, in the opposite direction, securing the bead in a horizontal (rather than vertical) direction. (Fig. B)

3. Repeat this process with 2 more gold tube beads, stringing each one onto one cord in one direction, and onto the other cord in the other direction. (Fig. C)

4. Repeat this process to string a total of 16 gold tube beads on one side of the bracelet. Measure the bracelet to make sure that it is almost half of the desired length. If not, add a few more beads (and remember to add them to the other side, too).

5. String the smaller rhinestone and gold button onto the cords in the same manner in which you strung the tube beads, stringing each cord through the button hole in the opposite direction. (Fig. D)

6. Now string the remaining 16 tube beads on the cords, in the same manner as before. Add more tube beads to this side of the bracelet if you added extra beads on the first side. Tie a double knot at the end of the bracelet, flush against the last tube bead. (Fig. E)

7. String the larger rhinestone and gold button onto one of the bracelet tails. String the other tail through the button hole in the opposite direction, and then tie the tails together in a double knot. Trim the ends about ¼" from the knot and melt the ends. Apply a drop or two of glue to secure the knot in place. (Fig. F)

Chic Checkerboard Bracelet

This bracelet combines lovely knots with pretty striped beads. Making the knots even in size takes a bit of practice, but once you've nailed the technique, you'll find it easy and useful!

Materials & Tools
(Fig. A)

- **Black waxed cord**
- **Tape**
- **6 round silver beads, 3 mm**
- **5 black and white cylinder beads, 4 mm**
- **1 black seed bead, 8/0**
- **1 yellow seed bead, 8/0**
- **1 red seed bead, 8/0**
- **1 silver seed bead, 8/0**
- **Scissors**
- **Lighter**

40 minutes

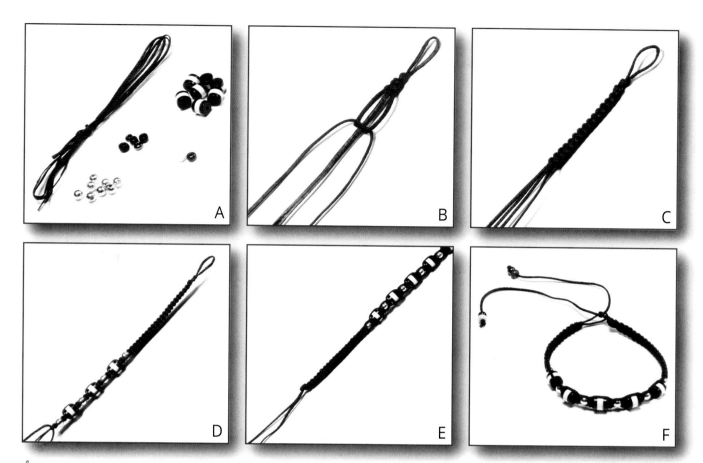

1. Cut a 20" piece of black waxed cord, fold it in half, and tie an overhand knot at the folded end of the cord to form a ¼" loop. These will be the base cords of your bracelet. Tape the loop to a tabletop to hold it in place. Cut a 5" piece of waxed cord and place the middle of it just below the overhand knot. Make sure the cord extends evenly on either side of the base cords. These will be the tying cords. Tie 2 square knots in the tying cords, anchoring them to the base cords. Continue tying square knots over the base cords. (Fig. B)

2. When you have tied 22 knots over the base cords, measure the bracelet to make sure it is about one-third of the desired length. If necessary, make a few more knots. (Fig. C)

3. String 1 round silver bead onto the base cords and draw it up so that it is

flush with the last square knot. Draw the tying cords around the bead and tie them in 2 square knots after the bead, securing it in place. String 1 black and white cylinder bead onto the base cords. Draw the tying cords around the bead and tie them in 2 square knots after the bead.

4. Repeat this process 2 more times, alternately stringing silver beads and black and white cylinder beads, and tying 2 square knots between each bead. String on 1 silver bead and tie 2 square knots over the base cords. (Fig. D)

5. Continue this pattern until you have strung a total of 6 silver beads and 5 black and white cylinder beads. Make sure to tie 2 square knots between each bead. Tie 22 square knots after the last silver bead. Add more knots to this side of the bracelet if you added extra knots

previously, so that the first and last third of the bracelet are even in length. Tie the tying cords in a double knot over the base cords. Leave the base cords long and trim the tying cords to ¼" from the knot. Melt the ends. (Fig. E)

6. String a black seed bead and a yellow seed bead onto one of the base cords. Tie a knot about 3" from the last square knot of the bracelet, and then trim the end to ¼" and melt it. String a red seed bead and a silver seed bead onto the other base cord. Tie a knot about 3" from the last square knot of the bracelet, and then trim the end to ¼" and melt it.

7. To secure this bracelet, draw one of the base cords through the loop you made at the beginning and tie it in a knot with the other base cord. (Fig. F)

Pretty-in-Peace Bracelet

In this bright bracelet, both the beads and the waxed cords are colorful and bright. You can line up all the peace beads so that they face the same direction, or let one of them face the other direction to make it more interesting.

Materials & Tools
(Fig. A)
- Brown waxed cord
- 1 yellow peace bead, 10 mm
- 1 turquoise peace bead, 10 mm
- 1 pink peace bead, 10 mm
- Tape
- Turquoise waxed cord
- 2 yellow seed beads, 8/0
- 2 turquoise seed beads, 8/0
- Scissors
- Lighter

35 minutes

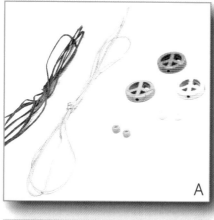

A

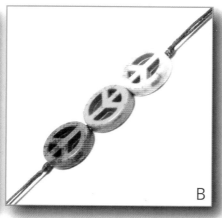

B

C

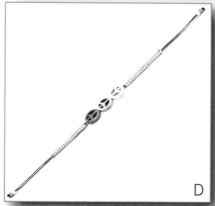

D

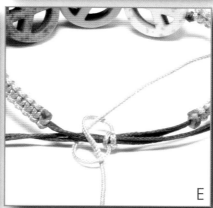

E

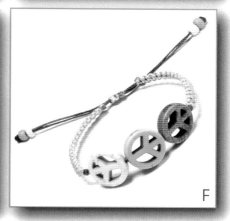

F

1. Cut two 20" pieces of brown waxed cord. String the yellow peace bead onto both cords, drawing it up towards the middle of the cords. String the turquoise and pink peace beads next, in whatever direction you choose. Draw all three beads to the middle of the brown cords. Tie overhand knots in the cords at both ends of the beads to secure them in place. (Fig. B) Tape the cords extending from the yellow peace bead to a tabletop to hold the bracelet in place.

2. Cut a 16" piece of turquoise waxed cord and draw it behind the cords extending from the pink peace bead. Arrange the cord so that the right and left sides of it are even. The brown cords will be the base cords and the turquoise cords will be the tying cords. Make 1 square knot with the turquoise tying cords to secure them in place. (Fig. C)

3. Continue making square knots on this side of the bracelet until you have 18 square knots. Measure the bracelet to make sure these knots make up about one-third of the desired length. If necessary, make a few more knots. When this side of the bracelet is the right length, tie the turquoise tying cords in a double knot over the base cords. Trim the turquoise cords to ¼" from the double knot and melt the ends.

4. Repeat this process on the other side of the peace beads. Add more knots to this side of the bracelets if you added extra knots previously. Trim the ends of the turquoise tying cords to ¼" and melt them. (Fig. D)

5. Cut an 8" piece of turquoise cord. Wrap the tails of the bracelet over each other in opposite directions and place the 8" piece of cord under them. Tie the cord in a square knot over the tails of the bracelet, holding them in place. (Fig. E)

6. Tie another 4 square knots in the turquoise cord, making a closure for the bracelet. Trim the cords about ¼" from the last square knot and then melt the ends. String 1 yellow seed bead and 1 turquoise seed bead on one bracelet tail. Tie an overhand knot in the tail after the turquoise bead, about 2" from the last knot in the bracelet. Repeat on the other bracelet tail.

7. Trim the cords about ¼" from the knot and then melt the ends. (Fig. F)

He-Sells-Seashells Bracelet

This colorful bracelet is a great summertime keepsake. You might not be able to find perfect shells on the beach, but you can certainly order some online. The bright waxed cord and colorful wooden beads complete the sunny summertime effect.

Materials & Tools
(Fig. A)

- **Yellow waxed cord**
- **Tape**
- **14 flat wooden disk beads, various colors, 4 mm**
- **3 cowrie shell beads, 8 mm**
- **1 fuchsia seed bead, 8/0**
- **1 turquoise seed bead, 8/0**
- **1 metallic pink seed bead, 8/0**
- **1 yellow seed bead, 8/0**
- **Scissors**
- **Lighter**

60
minutes

A

B

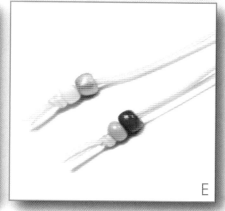

C

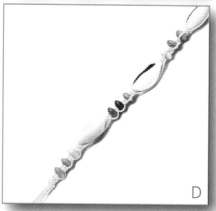

D

E

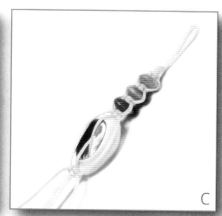

F

1. Cut a 20" piece of yellow waxed cord, fold it in half, and tie an overhand knot at the folded end of the cord to form a ¼" loop. These will be the base cords of your bracelet. Tape the loop to a tabletop to hold it in place. Cut a 5" piece of yellow waxed cord and draw it behind the looped cord, close to the overhand knot. Arrange the cord so that the right and left sides of it are even. These will be the tying cords. Use the tying cords to make 2 square knots over the base cords. (Fig. B)

2. String 1 flat wooden disk bead onto the base cords and draw it up to the square knots. Bring the tying cords around the bead and tie them in 2 square knots after the bead, securing it in place.

3. Repeat this process another 2 times to string 2 more flat wooden disk beads onto the base cords. String on 1 cowrie shell bead and then make 2 square knots after it over the base cords. (Fig. C)

4. Repeat this process to string 3 more sets of 3 flat wooden disk beads, interspersed with 2 shell beads. Make 2 square knots after the last wooden disk bead. Gather all 4 cords together and tie them in a secure overhand knot that is flush with the last square knots. (Fig. D)

5. Hold 2 of the cords together, and string on 1 fuchsia seed bead and 1 turquoise seed bead. Make an overhand knot in these cords, about 4" from the last overhand knot.

6. Trim the ends to ¼" and melt the ends to make one bracelet tail. Hold the other 2 cords together, and string on 1 metallic pink seed bead and 1 yellow seed bead. Make an overhand knot in these cords, about 4" from the last square knot. Trim the ends to ¼" and melt the ends to make the other bracelet tail. (Fig. E)

7. The closure in this bracelet is made by drawing one of the bracelet tails through the loop you made at the beginning and tying it in a knot with the other bracelet tail. (Fig. F)

Enchanting Seas Bracelet

This beautiful bracelet has a bit of sparkle and a bit of edge, plus several gorgeous shades of blue. I recommend using pliers to fold over the stud prongs, but if you don't have any on hand, you can use a blunt knife or thimble.

Materials & Tools
(Fig. A)

- 2 rhinestone silver chains, each 4" long
- 1 blue knotted bracelet, 4" long
- Blue embroidery floss
- 3 textured silver cone prong studs
- Glue
- Needle
- Scissors
- Pliers

  60 minutes

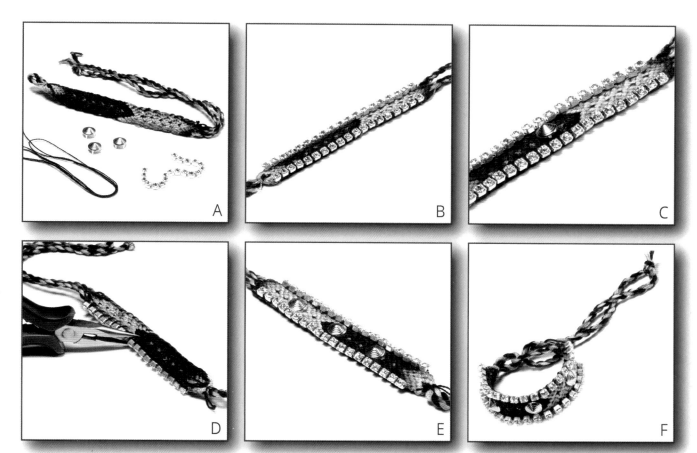

1. Lay 1 rhinestone chain along the left side of the blue knotted bracelet. Thread a needle with blue embroidery floss and make a knot at one end of the floss. Secure the chain along the side of the bracelet by sewing overcast stitches along the length of the chain, one stitch between every rhinestone. Tie a double knot in the floss, on the backside of the bracelet, and trim the ends. Apply a dot of glue to affix the knot to the backside of the bracelet.

2. Lay the other rhinestone silver chain along the other side of the bracelet and sew it into place. (Fig. B)

3. Place one silver cone prong stud on the center of the bracelet. (Fig. C)

4. Press it down so that the prongs come out the backside of the bracelet, and then fold over the prongs, using pliers. (Fig. D)

5. Place a silver cone prong stud on either side of the stud you secured previously, making sure the two studs are equidistant from the two ends of the bracelet. Press down on each stud so that the prongs come out the backside of the bracelet, and then fold over the prongs, using pliers. (Fig. E)

6. The closure for this bracelet is made by drawing one of the bracelet ends through the loop in the bracelet and tying it in a knot with the other bracelet end. (Fig. F)

LOVE-is-a-Rainbow Bracelet

This lovely bracelet is an amazing example of how you can dress up a readymade knotted bracelet with ease. As for the charm you sew on, choose any phrase you connect with!

Materials & Tools
(Fig. A)

- 1 rhinestone and gold LOVE charm, with loops
- 1 rainbow knotted bracelet, 4" long
- Blue embroidery floss
- Glue
- Needle
- Scissors

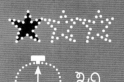

30 minutes

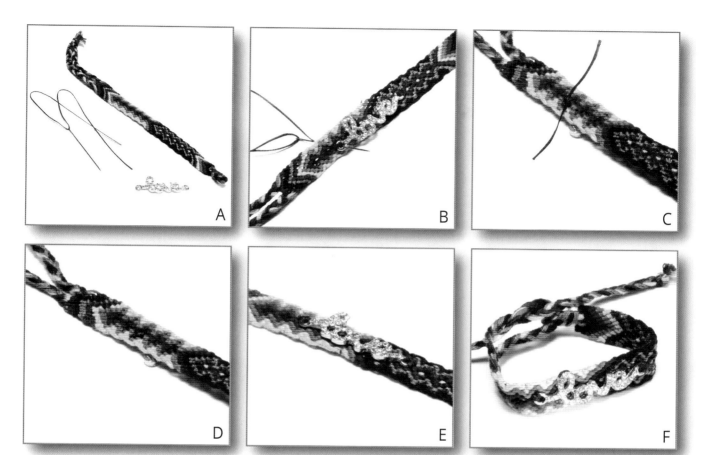

1. Place the LOVE charm on the center of the rainbow knotted bracelet. Thread a needle with blue embroidery floss and make a knot at one end of the floss. Secure the charm at one side by sewing a few overcast stitches through one loop in the charm to connect it to the knotted bracelet. Tie a double knot in the floss on the backside of the bracelet. Trim the ends of the floss, and apply a dot of glue to affix the knot to the backside of the bracelet.

2. Make a few overcast stitches through the loop on the other side of the charm, securing it to the bracelet. (Fig. B)

3. Tie a double knot in the floss on the backside of the bracelet. (Fig. C)

4 Trim the ends of the floss, and apply a dot of glue to affix the knot to the backside of the bracelet. (Fig. D)

5. Apply a few drops of glue to the bottom of the charm to secure it in place. (Fig. E)

6. The closure for this bracelet is made by drawing one of the bracelet ends through the loop in the bracelet and tying it in a knot with the other bracelet end. (Fig. F)

Lucky Jade Band

This colorful bracelet features a multicolored embroidered band, soft leather wristband and a jade stone donut. It's a great way of transforming a non-adjustable embroidered band into an adjustable bracelet!

Materials & Tools
(Fig. A)

- 1 multicolored embroidered band, 5" x ½"
- 1 blue leather wristband, 8" x ½", with 2 gold snaps
- Jade stone donut, 15 mm
- Turquoise waxed cord
- Glue
- Needle
- Lighter

20
minutes

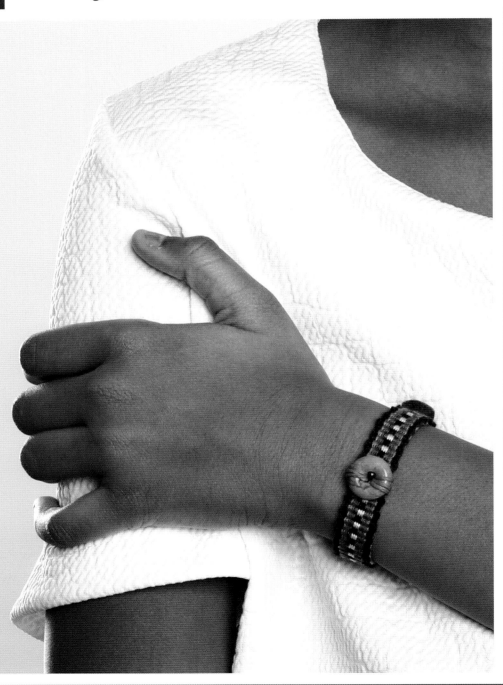

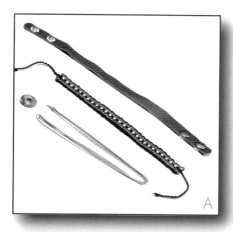

A

B

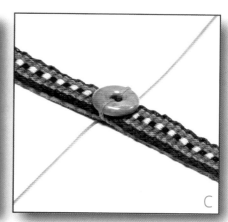

C

D

E

F

1. Place the multicolored embroidered bracelet on the blue leather wristband. Make sure the right side of the embroidered bracelet is facing upwards, and fits evenly between the snaps on the leather wristband. When you are satisfied with the placement of the embroidered band, apply glue to the backside of the embroidered bracelet and affix on the wristband.

2. Place the jade stone donut on the center of the bracelet. You can measure, if you like, to make sure the position is just right. (Fig. B)

3 Thread a needle with turquoise waxed cord. Insert the needle into the bracelet, from the backside to the front, through the middle of the donut. Pull the cord through so that a long tail remains at the back of the bracelet. Wrap the cord around one side of the donut and around the edge of the wristband, and bring the needle back up through the middle of the donut.

4. Repeat the process, this time wrapping the cord around the other side of the jade donut. (Fig. C)

5. When the jade donut is secured to the bracelet, bring the ends of the cord together at the backside of the wristband and tie them in a secure double knot. (Fig. D)

6. Affix the knot to the backside of the bracelet with a dot of glue. Trim the cords to about ¼" from the knot and then melt the ends. (Fig. E)

7. The closure on this bracelet is adjustable, and can be closed on either one of the two snaps. (Fig. F)

Peace and Friendship Bracelet

Add some glitter to a standard knotted bracelet with a sparkling peace charm. Of course, you can choose any type of charm you like – just make sure it is sparkly, fun and a sign of your friendship!

Materials & Tools
(Fig. A)
- **1 rhinestone and silver peace charm**
- **1 rainbow knotted bracelet, 4" long**
- **Pink embroidery floss**
- **Glue**
- **Needle**
- **Scissors**

25 minutes

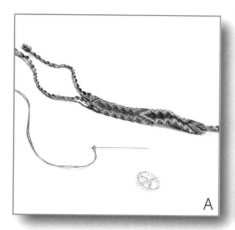

A

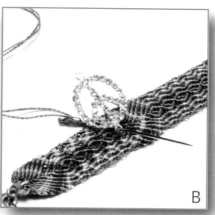

B

C

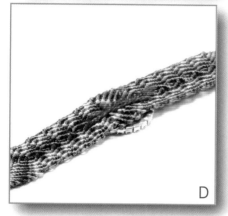

D

E

F

1. Place the peace charm on the center of the rainbow knotted bracelet. Thread a needle with pink embroidery floss and make a knot at one end of the floss. Insert the needle into the bracelet, from the backside to the front, through the loop at the top of the peace charm. (Fig. B) Wrap the floss around the loop and back into the bracelet to secure the peace charm in place.

2. Repeat a few more times to secure the top of the peace charm. (Fig. C)

3. Draw the floss along the backside of the bracelet and push it out near the bottom of the peace charm. Wrap the floss around the peace charm several times to secure it in place, and then tie the floss in a secure double knot at the backside of the bracelet. Trim the floss ends, and apply a dot of glue to secure the knot to the backside of the bracelet. (Fig. D)

4. Apply a few drops of glue to the bottom of the peace charm if you like, to secure it in place. (Fig. E)

5. The closure for this bracelet is made by drawing one of the bracelet ends through the loop in the bracelet and tying it in a knot with the other bracelet end. (Fig. F)

Embellished Earthy Bracelet

Dress up a standard earth-colored knotted bracelet with some golden rhinestones and a stud. The changes are simple but the results really stand out.

Materials & Tools
(Fig. A)

- **1 textured gold cone prong stud**
- **1 earth-tone knotted bracelet, 4" long**
- **5 brown glue-on rhinestones**
- **Glue**
- **Pliers**

25 minutes

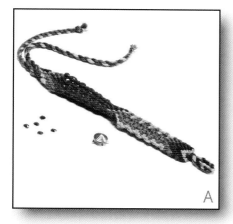

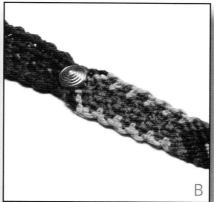

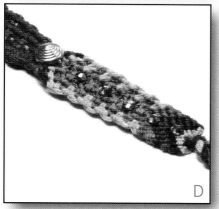

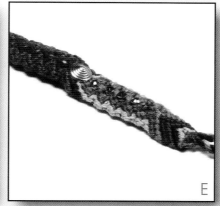

1. Place the stud on the center of the knotted bracelet. (Fig. B)

2. Press it down so that the prongs come out the backside of the bracelet, and then fold over the prongs using pliers. (Fig. C)

3. Arrange the rhinestones on the bracelet at equal intervals, between the stud in the middle of the bracelet and the loop at one end. (Fig. D)

4. When you are satisfied with the rhinestone arrangement, apply a drop of glue to the back of each rhinestone and affix them to the bracelet. (Fig. E)

5. The closure for this bracelet is made by drawing one of the bracelet ends through the loop in the bracelet and tying it in a knot with the other bracelet end. (Fig. F)

Leather LOVE Band

This design combines a hard rock center with a soft leather wristband. Make sure you have a leather hole punch, sturdy needle, and durable multipurpose glue.

Materials & Tools
(Fig. A)

- **1 gold LOVE charm**
- **1 stone bead, 1½" x ½"**
- **Glue**
- **1 beige leather wristband, 8" x ½", with 2 gold snaps**
- **Brown waxed cord**
- **Fine marker**
- **Leather hole punch**
- **Scissors**
- **Needle**

15 minutes

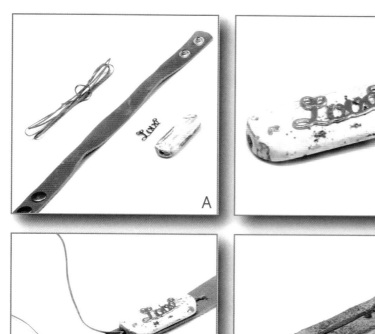

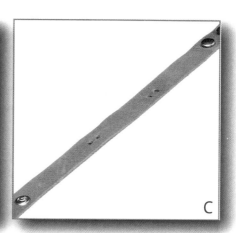

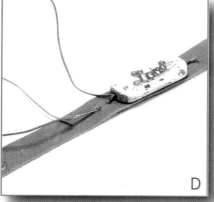

1. Place the gold LOVE charm on top of the stone bead. When you are satisfied with the position of the letters, apply drops of glue to the backside of the charm and affix it to the bead. (Fig. B)

2. Place the stone bead on the center of the leather wristband. Mark a dot at each end of the stone bead with a fine marker. Remove the stone bead from the wristband, and mark a dot ¼" to the right of the dot on the right side. Mark another dot ¼" to the left of the dot on the left side. Punch holes in the four dots, using the leather hole punch. (Fig. C)

3. Apply glue to the backside of the stone bead and affix it to the middle of the leather wristband. Let it sit for

about 10 minutes to allow the glue to dry. Cut an 8" piece of brown waxed cord. Thread the needle with the cord and insert it from the backside of the bracelet towards the front, into one of the holes that is closest to a snap. Leave a 2" tail at the backside, for tying later.

4. Insert the needle back down into the adjacent hole, and then draw it up again through the first hole and insert it into the stone bead. Draw out the needle from the other side of the stone bead, insert it into the hole that's closest to the bead, and then draw it upwards through the adjacent hole. Draw the cord back through the bead and out the other side. Insert the needle down through the hole closest to the snap. (Fig. D)

5. Draw it under the bracelet to the hole closest to the bead, and then draw the cord through the bead again.

6. Repeat this process another two times, securing the stone bead in place. When the stone bead is securely affixed, tie the cord in a secure double knot on the backside of the bracelet. Trim the tails to about ¼" from the knot and then melt the ends. Add a drop of glue to secure the tails. (Fig. E)

7. The closure on this bracelet is adjustable, and can be closed on either one of the two snaps. (Fig. F)

Fun Floral Wristband

This colorful wristband features a floral centerpiece, lovely criss-crosses and a soft leather wristband. The possible color combinations are endless, but make sure you choose a leather wristband that is just the right size.

Materials & Tools
(Fig. A)

- 1 multicolored embroidered band, 5" x ½"
- 1 gray leather wristband, 8" x ½", with 2 gold snaps
- 1 embroidered flower, 1½" x 1½"
- Glue
- Tape
- Blue waxed cord
- Scissors

60
minutes

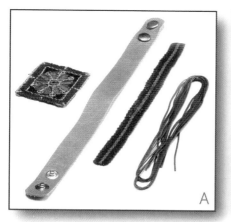

A

B

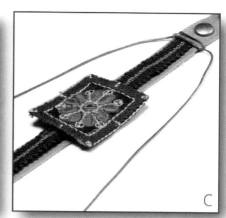

C

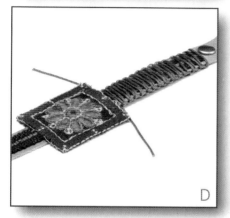

D

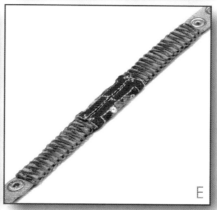

E

F

1. Place the multicolored embroidered band on the gray leather wristband. Make sure the right side of the band is facing upwards, and position the band so that it fits between the snaps on the leather wristband.

2. Apply glue to the backside of the embroidered band and affix it onto the leather wristband. Place the embroidered flower in the middle of the bracelet. Apply glue only to the middle of the backside of the embroidered flower (not the left and right sides) and affix it to the embroidered band. (Fig. B)

3. Tape one end of the leather wristband to a tabletop to hold it in place. Cut a 3" piece of blue waxed cord and draw it behind the leather

wristband, just below the gold snaps. Arrange the cord so that the left and right sides of it are even. Make a square knot in the cord to secure it around the leather wristband. (Fig. C)

4. Continue making square knots along the bracelet until you reach the embroidered flower in the middle. (Fig. D)

5. Rotate the leather wristband and tape the other end of it to the tabletop. Cut another 3" piece of blue waxed cord and repeat the process of tying it to the other side of the bracelet. Fold all 4 cord tails onto the back of the bracelet, immediately behind the embroidered flower, and affix them with a few dots of glue.

6. Apply a generous amount of glue to the left and right backsides of the embroidered flower, and then fold the two sides over the cord tails to conceal them. Press down the sides of the embroidered flower until they are affixed. (Fig. E)

7. The closure on this bracelet is adjustable, and can be closed on either one of the two snaps. (Fig. F)

This sparkly bracelet has a touch of earthiness too, thanks to its soft leather backing. As for the colors, turquoise and orange are complementary colors that look amazing together.

Materials & Tools
(Fig. A)

- **2 blue rhinestone silver chains, each 5" long**
- **1 beige leather wristband, 8" x ½", with 2 gold snaps**
- **Glue**
- **Tape**
- **Orange waxed cord**
- **Scissors**
- **Lighter**

25 minutes

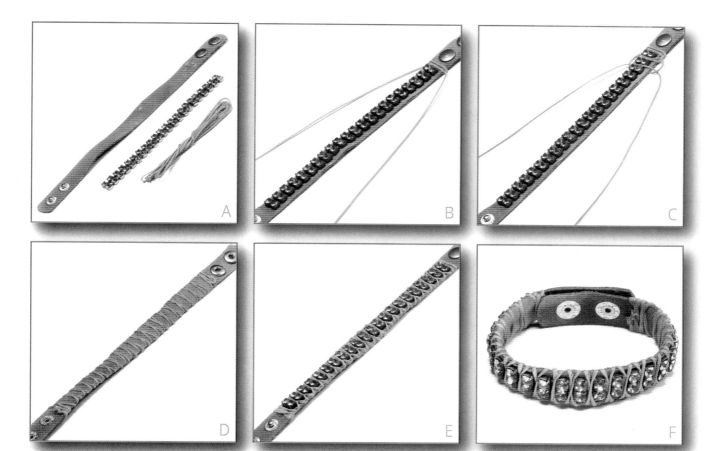

1. Lay both rhinestone chains along the middle of the beige leather wristband. Make sure the chains are centered between the snaps. Apply glue to the backside of the chains and affix them onto the leather wristband. Let them sit for about 10 minutes to allow the glue to dry.

2. Tape one end of the wristband to a tabletop to hold it in place. Cut a 5" piece of orange waxed cord. Fold it in half and attach it at the taped end of the wristband, between the gold snaps and the rhinestone chains, with a lark's head knot. Draw the knot to the backside of the wristband, and draw one piece of cord to each side of the wristband. (Fig. B)

3. Grasp the cord on the right and wrap it over the front of the wristband, between the first and second pair of rhinestone chains. Draw the cord on a diagonal and wrap it around the left side of the wristband and around the back. Bring the cord to the front of the wristband on the right side, between the second and third pair of rhinestones. Wrap it over the front of the wristband, this time between the second and third pair of rhinestones. Draw the cord on a diagonal and wrap it around the back of the wristband. (Fig. C)

4. Repeat this process all the way to the other end of the wristband, first wrapping the cord on the right side and

then wrapping the cord on the left side. When both cords have been wrapped along the length of the wristband, bring them to the backside of the wristband and tie them in a secure double knot. Trim the ends to about ¼" from the knot and then melt the ends. Apply a drop of glue to secure the knot in place. (Fig. D)

5. Arrange the cords so they are wrapped evenly between the rhinestones and apply a drop or two of glue to secure them in place, if required. (Fig. E)

6. The closure on this bracelet is adjustable, and can be closed on either one of the two snaps. (Fig. F)

ZigZag Pizzazz Bracelet

This bracelet has so much going for it— gorgeous turquoise teardrops, sparkly rhinestone and gold link chains, gorgeous knotted bracelets and a soft leather wristband.

Materials & Tools
(Fig. A)

- **2 rhinestone silver chains, each 3½" long**
- **2 colorful knotted bracelets, each 3½" long**
- **Blue embroidery floss**
- **Glue**
- **1 gold link chain, 3" long**
- **1 beige leather wristband, 8" x ½", with 2 gold snaps**
- **10 gold jump rings, 6 mm**
- **10 turquoise teardrop beads, 10 mm**
- **Needle**
- **Scissors**
- **Pliers**

60
minutes

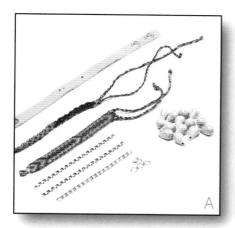

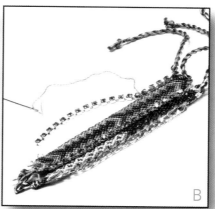

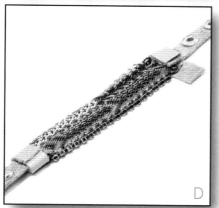

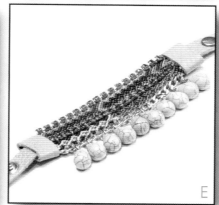

1. Lay 1 rhinestone chain along one side of a knotted bracelet. Thread a needle with blue embroidery floss and make a knot at one end of the floss. Secure the chain along the side of the bracelet by sewing overcast stitches along the length of the chain, one stitch between every rhinestone. Tie a double knot in the floss, on the backside of the bracelet, and trim the ends. Apply a dot of glue to affix the knot to the backside of the bracelet. Lay the other knotted bracelet alongside the first bracelet, so that the rhinestone chain is between the two knotted bracelets.

2. Connect the bracelets by sewing overcast stitches between each rhinestone in the chain, this time in the opposite direction. Tie a double knot at the end of the floss, on the backside of the bracelets, and secure with a dot of glue. Lay the gold link chain along the outer edge of one of

the knotted bracelets. Connect the chain to the bracelet by sewing overcast stitches between every link in the chain. Lay the other rhinestone chain along the outer edge of the other knotted bracelet and connect to the bracelet by sewing overcast stitches between every rhinestone. (Fig. B)

3. Trim the tail ends of the knotted bracelets. Cut the leather wristband in half, and then cut each half in half again. Take a strip of leather without any snaps and affix it at one end of the knotted bracelets, perpendicular to the bracelets and covering the ends. Apply glue only to the middle back of the leather strip, and affix it on the top of the bracelets. Leave the ends unglued for now.

4. Take a leather strip with snap tops and affix it with glue directly under the leather strip you affixed previously. Make

sure the snaps are facing in the right direction. (Fig. C)

5. Now apply glue on the backside of the top and bottom of the first leather strip and fold them over the leather strip with the snaps, securing it firmly in place. Let it sit for about 10 minutes to allow the glue to dry. Repeat this process on the other side of the bracelet to affix the leather strip with the snap bottoms. (Fig. D)

6. Use the pliers to open a jump ring. String a turquoise teardrop bead onto the jump ring and string it onto a link on the chain. Close the jump ring. Repeat this process to string all of the turquoise beads onto jump rings, and then onto the gold chain. (Fig. E)

7. The closure on this bracelet is adjustable, and can be closed on either one of the two snaps. (Fig. F)

Elegant Emerald Bracelet

This relaxing design features a cool green oval centerpiece and soft leather wristband. I've used green waxed cord to secure the center, but you could use a complementary color too.

Materials & Tools
(Fig. A)

- 1 gold flat rectangular plate, with 2 holes
- 1 beige leather wristband, 8" x ½", with 2 gold snaps
- Glue
- Green waxed cord
- 1 flat oval faceted green bead, 10 mm
- Fine marker
- Leather hole punch
- Scissors
- Needle
- Lighter

15 minutes

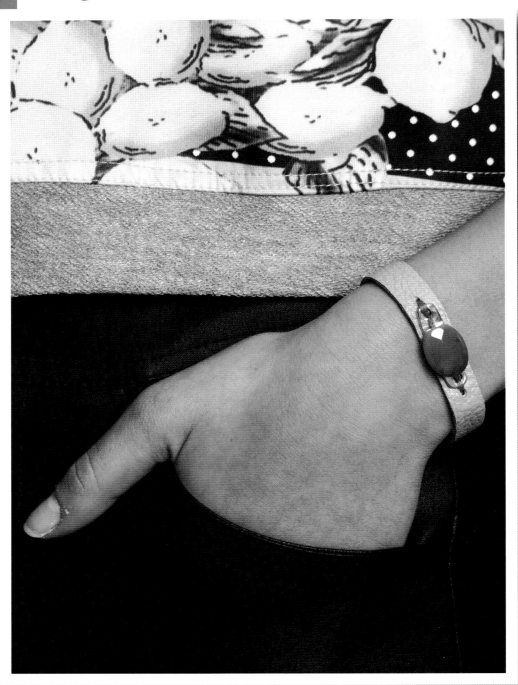

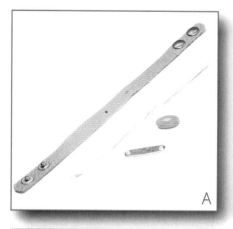

A

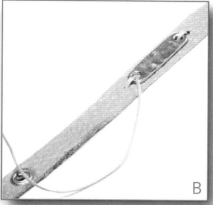

B

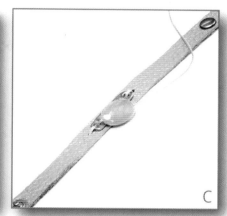

C

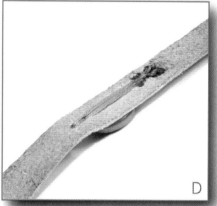

D

E

F

1. Place the gold plate on the center of the leather wristband. Using a fine marker, mark the position of the holes in the gold plate on the leather wristband. Remove the plate and mark two more holes: one of them ¼" to the left of the left hole; and the other ¼" to the right of the right hole. Use the leather hole punch to punch holes in the marked locations. Place a drop of glue on the back of the gold plate and then affix it to the middle of the leather wristband.

2. Cut a 10" piece of green waxed cord. Thread the needle with the cord and insert it from the backside of the bracelet towards the front, through one of the holes in the gold plate as well. Leave a 2" tail at the back, for tying later. Wrap the cord around the edge of the gold plate and insert it into the adjacent hole on the leather wristband. Draw the cord along the backside of the bracelet

and draw it out through the hole at the other end of the gold plate. Insert cord into the adjacent hole in the leather wristband and draw the cord back along the backside of the bracelet to the first hole that you used. (Fig. B)

3. Bring the cord back up to the front of the bracelet and string on the green bead. Draw the bead down the cord until it is flush with the gold plate and then insert the cord into the other hole on the gold plate, securing the bead in place. (Fig. C)

4. Bring the cord back up through the adjacent hole in the leather wristband, then wrap the cord around the edge of the gold plate and insert it into the hole in the gold plate, and the hole in the wristband. Draw the cord along the backside of the bracelet, and push it up through the other hole in the gold plate.

Wrap the cord around the edge of the gold plate and back down through the leather wristband. Repeat this process a few times and then draw the cord to the other side of the gold plate and repeat on the other side. Draw the cord along the backside of the bracelet to the tail you left in previously.

5. Tie the tails in a tight double knot at the backside of the bracelet. Trim the tail ends to ¼" from the knot and melt the ends. Apply a dot of glue to affix the knot to the leather wristband. (Fig. D)

6. Apply a drop or two of glue if you like to secure the bead in place. (Fig. E)

7. The closure on this bracelet is adjustable, and can be closed on either one of the two snaps. (Fig. F)

Bright Orange Funk Band

This bright bracelet features a richly colored, orange chain and a delicate turquoise cord. If you'd like to try this design with other complementary colors, try purple with yellow, or red with green.

Materials & Tools
(Fig. A)

- 1 opaque coral crystal chain, 5" long
- 1 beige leather wristband, 8" x ½", with 2 gold snaps
- Glue
- Tape
- Turquoise waxed cord
- Scissors
- Lighter

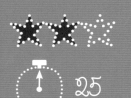

25 minutes

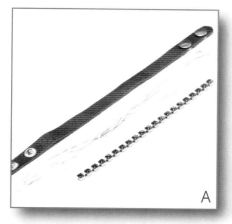

A

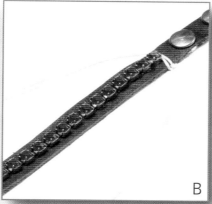

B

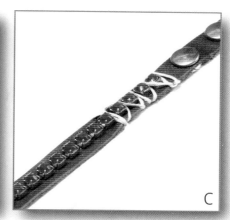

C

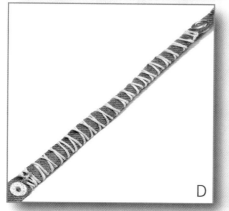

D

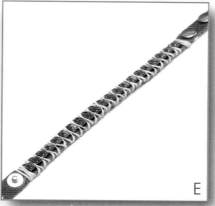

E

F

1. Lay the opaque coral crystal chain along the middle of the leather wristband. Make sure the chain is centered between the gold snaps. Apply glue to the backside of the chain and affix it to the leather wristband. Let it sit for about 10 minutes to allow the glue to dry. Tape one end of the wristband to a tabletop to hold it in place.

2. Cut a 5"piece of turquoise waxed cord. Fold it in half and attach it at the taped end of the wristband, between the gold snaps and the chain, with a lark's head knot. Draw the knot to the backside of the wristband, and draw one piece of cord to each side of the wristband. (Fig. B)

3. Grasp the cord on the right side and wrap it over the front of the wristband, between the first and second coral crystal. Draw the cord on a diagonal and wrap it around the left side of the wristband and around the back. Bring the cord to the front of the wristband on the right side, between the second and third coral crystal. Wrap it over the front of the wristband, this time between the second and third coral crystal. Draw the cord on a diagonal and wrap it around the back of the wristband.

4. Continue wrapping the cord on the right side of the wristband between coral crystals, and on a diagonal. After a few wraps, move to the cord on the left side of the wristband, and wrap this cord in the opposite direction between coral crystals, and the same number of times. (Fig. C)

5. Alternate between wrapping the two cords until you reach the other end of the wristband. Bring the cords to the backside of the bracelet and tie them in a secure double knot. Trim the cords about ¼" from the knot and then melt the ends. Apply a drop or two of glue to affix the knot to the leather wristband. (Fig. D)

6. Arrange the cords so they are wrapped evenly between the coral crystals. Apply a drop or two of glue to secure them in place, if required. (Fig. E)

7. The closure on this bracelet is adjustable, and can be closed on either one of the two snaps. (Fig. F)

Rainbow Wrap Bracelet

Jazz up a simple black leather cord by wrapping it with colorful waxed cord. This project requires absolutely no knotting, but it does require reliable glue, a sturdy clasp, and plenty of patience.

Materials & Tools
(Fig. A)

Glue

2 gold cord end caps, with holes, 4 mm

1 black leather cord, 6½" long, 4 mm

Light orange waxed cord

Dark orange waxed cord

Yellow waxed cord

Purple waxed cord

Tape

2 gold jump rings, 6 mm

1 gold lobster claw clasp

Scissors

Lighter

Pliers

40 minutes

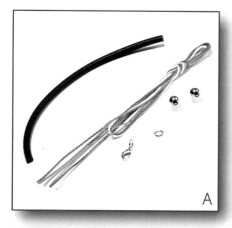

A

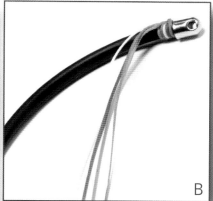

B

C

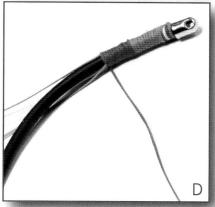

D

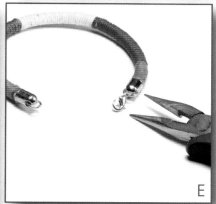

E

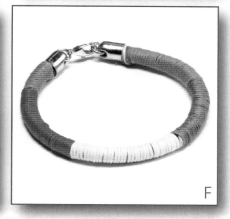

F

1. Place a few drops of glue into one gold cord end cap, and then tuck one end of the black leather cord into the end cap. Press firmly to affix. Cut 3½" pieces of light orange, dark orange, yellow and purple waxed cords. Line up the ends of the cords, and then wrap the cords around one end of the leather cord, adjacent to the cord end you affixed. Tie the cords in a double knot. (Fig. B)

2. Tape this end of the leather cord to a tabletop to hold it in place. Grasp the light orange cord in one hand and hold the three other cords flush against the leather cord in your other hand. Wrap the orange cord around the leather cord and the other cords several times, making the wraps close together so that they completely conceal the leather cord and the other waxed cords. (Fig. C)

3. Continue wrapping until you've covered about one-quarter of the leather cord with light orange cord. Now join the light orange cord with the other cords, hold it close to the leather cord, and draw the dark orange cord away from the rest. Start wrapping the dark orange cord around the leather cord, just as you did with the light orange cord. (Fig. D)

4. Continue wrapping until you are about halfway down the leather cord and then switch colors. Switch colors as often as you like, wrapping the waxed cords around the leather cord until you reach the end of the bracelet. Tie the 4 waxed cords together in a tight knot. Trim the cords about ¼" from the knot and then melt the ends. Apply a dot or two of glue to secure the knot.

5. Place a few drops of glue into the remaining gold cord end cap, and then tuck the other end of the leather cord into it. Press firmly to affix. Using pliers, open a gold jump ring and insert it into the hole in one of the cord end caps. String the clasp onto the jump ring and then close the jump ring. Open the other jump ring and string it onto the other cord end cap. String on the clasp and then close the jump ring. (Fig. E)

6. The closure for this bracelet is made with the clasp and the jump ring. (Fig. F)

Triple Wrap Rainbow Bracelet

Here's a glittering bracelet that's pretty and colorful. It wraps around the wrist three times, for a solid band of sparkly rainbow fun.

Materials & Tools
(Fig. A)

- **1 multicolored rhinestone chain, 14" long**
- **1 turquoise leather band, 15" x ¼"**
- **Glue**
- **Red embroidery floss**
- **Pink embroidery floss**
- **Blue embroidery floss**
- **Yellow embroidery floss**
- **Tape**
- **3" nylon macramé cord, rainbow (variegated) color**
- **Scissors**
- **Lighter**
- **Leather hole punch**

40 minutes

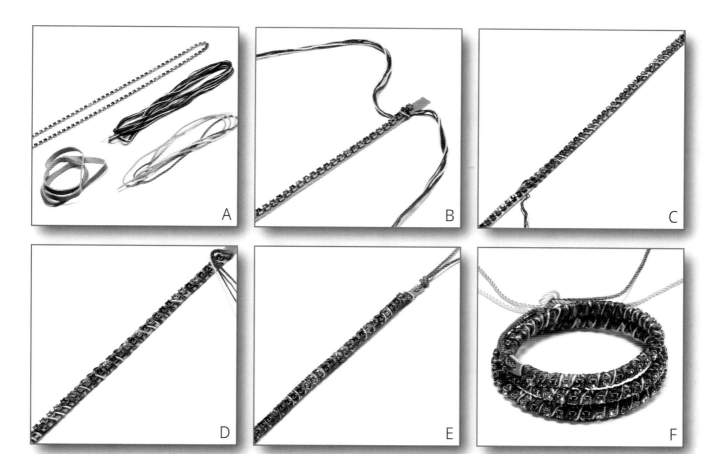

A

B

C

D

E

F

1. Lay the multicolored rhinestone chain along the middle of the turquoise leather band. Apply glue to the backside of the chain and affix it to the leather wristband. Let it sit for about 10 minutes to allow the glue to dry. Tape one end of the leather band to a tabletop to hold it in place.

2. Cut 12" pieces of red, pink, blue and yellow embroidery floss. Line up the ends and then fold the pieces in half. Attach them at the taped end of the leather band, immediately above the top rhinestone, with a lark's head knot. Draw the knot to the backside of the leather band and draw one piece of each color floss to each side of the band. (Fig. B)

3. Grasp all the floss pieces on the right side of the band and wrap them over the front of the band, between the first and second rhinestone. Draw the cords on a

diagonal and wrap them around the left side of the band and around the back. Bring these pieces of floss to the front of the bracelet, this time between the second and third rhinestone. Wrap them over the front of the bracelet, between the second and third rhinestone and draw them on a diagonal around the back of the band.

4. Repeat this process all the way down the bracelet, wrapping the embroidery floss on one side of the bracelet diagonally between each rhinestone. (Fig. C)

5. When you have reached the other end of the band, repeat this process with the pieces of embroidery floss on the left side of the bracelet. (Fig. D)

6. When you reach the other end of the bracelet with these pieces of

embroidery floss, bring all of the ends to the backside of the bracelet and tie them in a secure double knot. Trim the floss ends to about ¼" from the knot and apply a drop or two of glue to secure the knot to the band. Punch a hole at the top and bottom of the leather wristband, using the leather hole punch.

7. Cut the nylon macramé cord in half. String one of the pieces of nylon cord into one of the holes in the band, drawing it through the hole until both sides are even. Tie the cord in a knot close to the leather band to secure it in place. (Fig. E)

8. String the other piece of nylon cord into the other hole and secure with a knot close to the leather band. The closure for this bracelet is made by tying the nylon cords into a knot. (Fig. F)

Braided Rainbow Bracelet

This colorful bracelet is sparkly, fun and requires nothing more complicated than making a simple three-strand braid. The secret to its charm is the brightness of the materials. This bracelet is not adjustable, so make sure the combined length of the braided embroidery floss and the clasp are right.

Materials & Tools
(Fig. A)

- **8 pieces of embroidery floss, various colors, 5" each**
- **1 gold jump ring, 8 mm**
- **Glue**
- **1 rhinestone chain, 6½" long**
- **Tape**
- **1 gold lobster claw clasp**
- **Scissors**
- **Pliers**

40 minutes

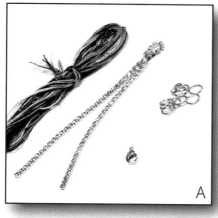

A

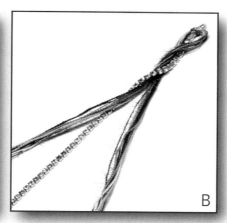

B

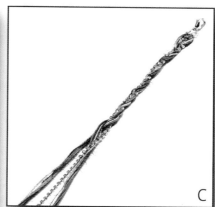

C

D

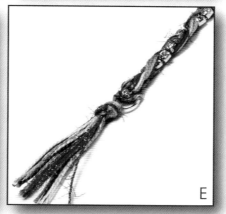

E

F

1. Grasp all of the pieces of embroidery floss so that they are lined up at one end. Insert the floss pieces through the gold jump ring and draw them through until the jump ring is in the middle. Tie the floss in a secure knot around the jump ring.

2. Divide the floss into two even groups and tie the two groups together in a knot. Apply a drop of glue to the knot and press on one end of the rhinestone chain, to affix. Arrange the groups of floss so that there is one on either side of the rhinestone chain. Tape the jump ring to a tabletop to hold it in place.

3. Start plaiting a three-strand braid with the two groups of floss and the rhinestone chain. (Fig. B)

4. Plait the three strands together until you reach the end of the rhinestone chain. (Fig. C)

5. Tie the end of the rhinestone chain and the ends of the embroidery floss into an overhand knot. Trim the ends of the floss to about 1" from the knot. (Fig. D)

6. Using the pliers, open the other jump ring and insert it into the knot at this end of the bracelet. (Fig. E)

7. String the clasp onto the jump ring and then close the jump ring.
The closure for this bracelet is made with the clasp and the jump ring. (Fig. F)

Positively Pink Tassel Bracelet

Here's a fun design, with a leather tassel centerpiece and funky gold chain. No knotting required, though it definitely has a cool knotted look to it.

Materials & Tools
(Fig. A)

Pink waxed cord

1 gold link chain, 6" long

Tape

1 pink leather and gold fringe

2 flat oval faceted transparent beads, 6 mm

Scissors

Lighter

25 minutes

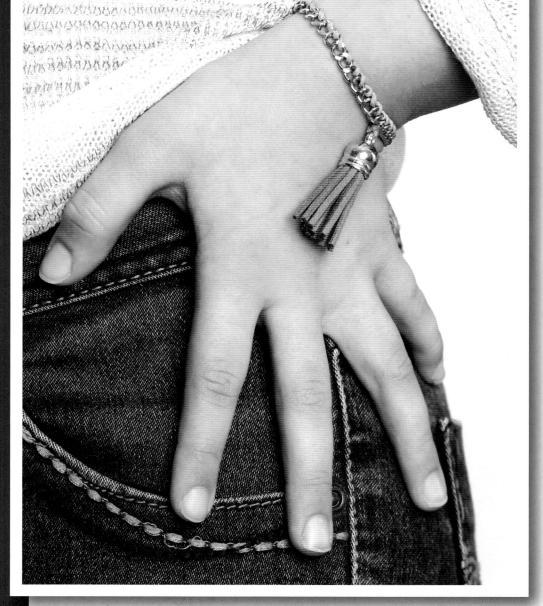

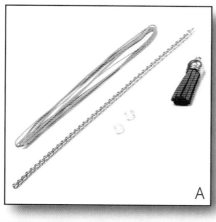

A

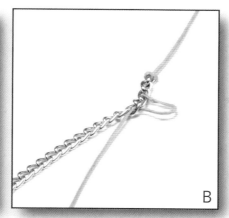

B

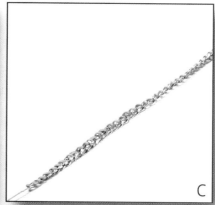

C

D

E

F

1. Cut a 10" piece of pink waxed cord and tie it to one end of the gold link chain, leaving a 3" tail. Tape this end of the gold link chain to a tabletop to hold it in place. Weave the cord in and out of the gold chain, one link at a time, by drawing it into one link and then out the next link. (Fig. B)

2. Repeat this process until you reach the other end of the gold chain, and then wrap the cord around the last link in the chain and tie a knot. Leave a 3" tail. (Fig. C)

3. Place the fringe at the middle of the cord-wrapped chain. Cut a 5" piece of pink waxed cord. Fold it in half and string the folded part of the cord through the loop at the top of the fringe, and then through the middle link in the chain.

4. Draw the ends of the cord through the loop at the top of the fringe to make a lark's head knot, and then tie a double knot in the cord to secure it in place. Trim the cords about ¼" from the knot and then melt the ends. (Fig. D)

5. Cut an 8" piece of waxed cord. Wrap the tails of the bracelet over each other in opposite directions, and place the 8" piece of cord under them. Tie the cord in a square knot over the tails of the bracelet, holding them in place. (Fig. E)

6. Tie 4 more square knots in the 8" piece of cord, making a closure for the bracelet. Trim the ends about ¼" from the last square knot and melt the ends. String 1 flat transparent bead on each bracelet tail. Make a knot after each bead, about 1½" from the closure. Trim the cords about ¼" from the knot and then melt the ends. (Fig. F)

Spunky Pink Band

This powerful pink bracelet really packs a punch. It's got fierce gold spikes and a hot pink band. Plus, it's really easy to make!

Materials & Tools
(Fig. A)

- **1 pink leather wristband, 8" x ½", with 2 gold snaps**
- **3 gold cone screw-on studs**
- **2 flat-topped glue-on studs**
- **Glue**
- **Leather hole punch**
- **Fine marker**

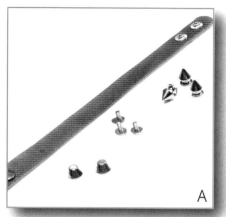

A

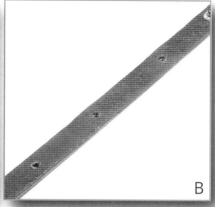

B

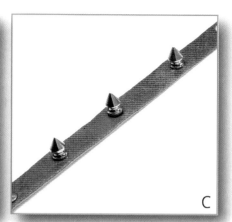

C

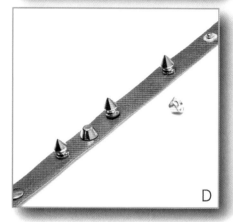

D

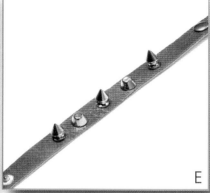

E

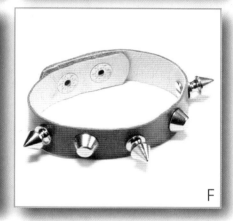

F

1. Using a leather hole punch, make a hole in the middle of the pink leather wristband. Make 2 more holes, one hole on either side of the hole you just made in the middle and equidistant from the gold snaps. (Fig. B)

2. Unscrew one of the gold cone screw-on studs. Insert the bottom of the stud, from the backside of the bracelet towards the front, in the middle hole. Screw on the top of the gold cone screw-on stud.

3. Repeat this process to screw on the other 2 gold cone studs. (Fig. C)

4. Using a fine marker, make a dot exactly between the middle and the left gold cone stud. You can measure, if you like, or simply estimate. Apply a drop of glue to the back of the flat-topped glue-on stud and affix it to the dot. (Fig. D)

5. Repeat this process on the other side of the bracelet, between the middle gold cone stud and right cone stud. (Fig. E)

6. The closure on this bracelet is adjustable, and can be closed on either one of the two snaps. (Fig. F)

Golden Good Fortune Bracelet

This solid design features a powerful collection of colors and materials. The smooth leather cord, shiny gold centerpiece and lucky charm centerpiece create a sense of elegance and inspiration.

Materials & Tools
(Fig. A)

- 1 black leather cord, 22" long, 2 mm
- 1 curved gold tube, 1" long, with loop
- Red waxed cord
- 2 gold seed beads, 8/0
- 2 red seed beads, 8/0
- 1 red eye charm
- Scissors
- Lighter
- Pliers

25 minutes

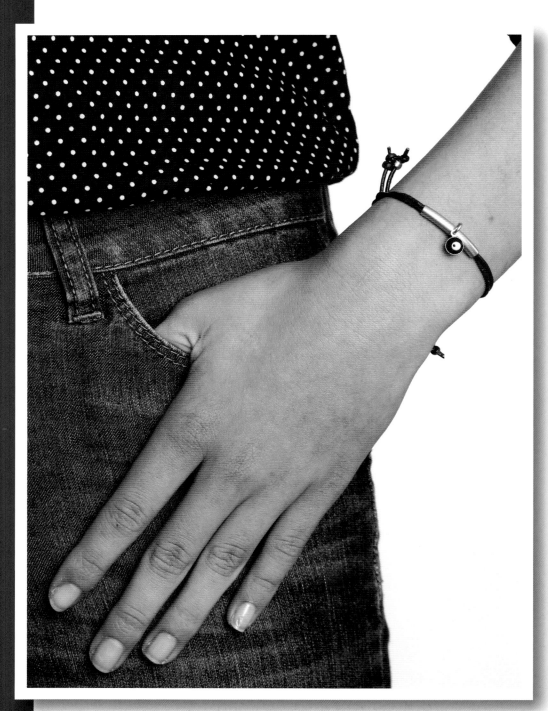

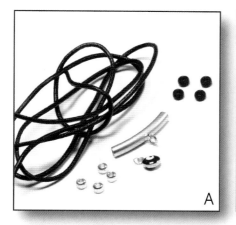

A

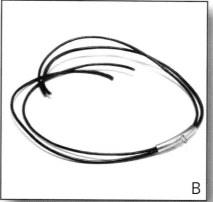

B

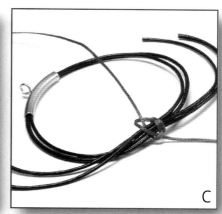

C

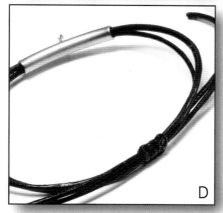

D

E

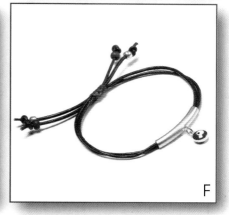

F

1. Cut the black leather cord in half. String both halves through the curved gold tube and draw the tube to the middle of the cords. (Fig. B)

2. Cut an 8" piece of red waxed cord. Wrap the black leather cord ends over each other in opposite directions and place the red waxed cord under them. Tie the waxed cord in a square knot over the tails of the leather cord, holding them in place. (Fig. C)

3. Tie 4 more square knots in the waxed cord, making a closure for the bracelet. Trim the waxed cords about ¼" from the last square knot and then melt the ends. (Fig. D)

4. String 1 gold bead on one leather cord end and 1 red bead on other leather cord end. (Fig. E)

5. Tie an overhand knot at the end of each of these leather cord ends, securing the beads in place.

6. Repeat on the other side of the bracelet. Using the pliers, open the loop on the curved gold tube and string on the red eye charm. Close the loop. (Fig. F)

Wrapped Ball Chain Bracelet

Dress up a bracelet with a simple ball chain by folding it and wrapping it with colorful waxed cord. Note that the length of the finished bracelet is not adjustable, so make sure the combined length of the twisted chain, cord end and clasp are right.

Materials & Tools
(Fig. A)

1 gold ball chain, 13" long

Fuchsia waxed cord

Tape

1 gold crimp end cap, with loop

Glue

1 gold jump ring, 6 mm

1 gold lobster claw clasp

Scissors

Lighter

Pliers

30 minutes

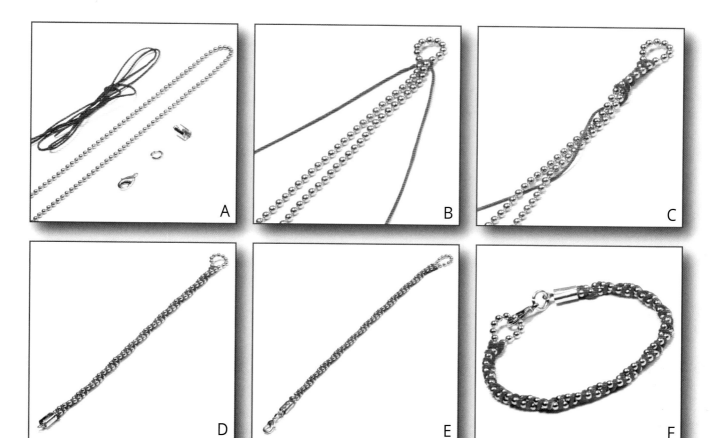

1. Fold the gold ball chain in half. Cut a 16" piece of fuchsia waxed cord and secure one end of it at the looped end of the chain with a double knot. Note that this loop is going to be part of the bracelet's clasp. (Fig. B)

2. Trim the tail of the cord to ¼" from the double knot and then melt the end. Tape the looped chain to a tabletop to hold it in place.

3. Wrap the cord around the folded gold ball chain, so that that it comes between each pair of gold balls, on a diagonal. Twist the gold chain as you wrap it, in the opposite direction as the wrapping. (Fig. C)

4. Continue wrapping until you reach the end of the gold chain, and then tie the cord in a double knot around the chain to secure it. Trim the cord about ¼" from the double knot and then melt it.

5. Place a few drops of glue into the gold crimp end cap. Tuck this end of the bracelet into the end cap and use the pliers to crimp the end cap closed. (Fig. D)

6. Open the jump ring and string it through the loop on the end cap. String the clasp onto the jump ring and then close the jump ring. (Fig. E)

7. The closure for this bracelet is made with the clasp and the jump ring. (Fig. F)

Cute-as-a-Button Bracelet

In this charming design, you'll use a cute turquoise button for the clasp and sturdy nylon cord for the bracelet. Make sure the loop you make in the nylon cord fits the button perfectly, and that the length is right for the wrist of the person you're making it for.

Materials & Tools
(Fig. A)
- 1 purple and pink (variegated) nylon macramé cord, 7"
- One 2-hole turquoise button, 10 mm
- Tape
- Glue
- Scissors
- Lighter

60 minutes

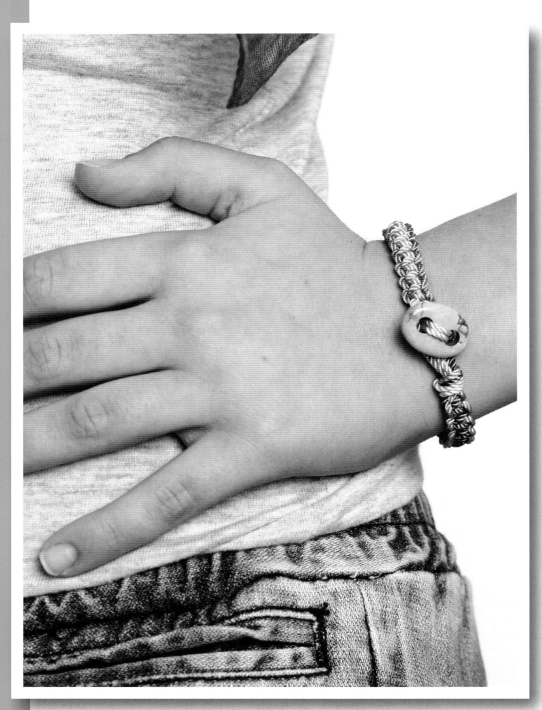

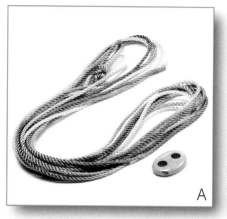

A

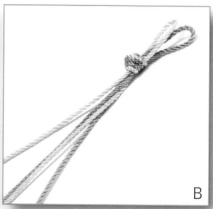

B

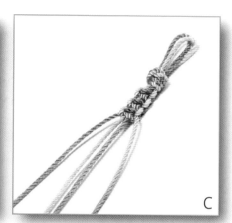

C

D

E

F

1. Cut the macramé cord in half and line up the ends. Fold the cords in half and tie an overhand knot at the folded end of the cords to form a loop. Make sure the loop is large enough to slip over the turquoise button. (Fig. B)

2. Tape the loop to a tabletop to hold it in place. Arrange the cords so that they lie flat on the table. The cords on the right and left side are the tying cords; the cords in the middle are the base cords. Start making square knots by knotting the tying cords over the base cords. (Fig. C)

3. Continue making square knots until the bracelet is the appropriate length. Draw one of the base cords into the left buttonhole, from the bottom upwards and insert it into the right buttonhole, from the top downwards.

4. Draw the other base cord into the right buttonhole, from the bottom upwards, and insert it into the left buttonhole, from the top downwards. Now both base cords should be strung through the buttonholes, in opposite directions. (Fig. D)

5. Hold the base cords close to the bracelet. Grasp the tying cords and wrap them around the base cords a few times to hold them in place, then tie them in a secure double knot. Trim the cords about ¼" from the knot and then melt the ends. Add a drop or two of glue to the knot to secure it. (Fig. E)

6. The closure for this bracelet is made by slipping the loops over the button. (Fig. F)

Twisted Knot Bracelet

This twisted knot bracelet may look like it requires careful knotting and lots of skill, but it doesn't really. Just two different waxed cord colors, and a simple knot pattern repeated over and over again.

Materials & Tools
(Fig. A)

- **Burgundy waxed cord**
- **Orange waxed cord**
- **Tape**
- **2 round faceted burgundy beads, 8 mm**
- **Scissors**
- **Lighter**

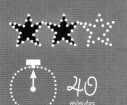

40 minutes

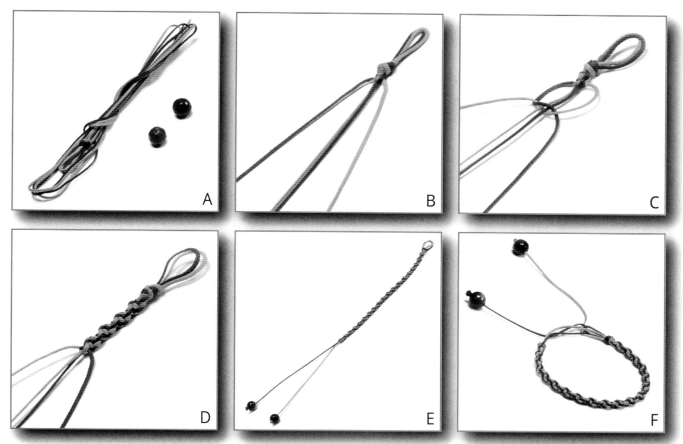

1. Cut a 40" piece of burgundy waxed cord and a 40" piece of orange waxed cord. Hold one end of each cord together and then fold the cords in half. Make an overhand knot at the looped end of the cords, making sure that the loop that you make is large enough for one of the burgundy beads to fit through. (Fig. B)

2. Tape the loop to a tabletop to hold it in place. Arrange the 4 cords so that one cord of each color is on the inside, as base cords, and one cord of each color is on the outside, as tying cords.

3. Bring the rightmost orange cord under the base cords and over the leftmost burgundy cord. Bring the leftmost burgundy cord over the base cords and under the rightmost orange cord. (Fig. C)

4. Repeat this process several times to create a chain of twisted French knots. (Fig. D)

5. Continue making French knots until the bracelet is the desired length. Tie the shorter orange and shorter burgundy cords (the tying cords) in a secure double knot. Trim the cords about ¼" from the knot and then melt the ends.

6. String 1 burgundy bead on each of the base cords and then make a knot after each bead, about 3" from the last French knot. Trim the cords about ¼" from the last knot and melt the ends. (Fig. E)

7. The closure for this bracelet is made by drawing one of the base cords through the loops you made at the beginning and tying it in a knot with the other base cord. (Fig. F)

Index

Models' clothes by

Amelli's Girl Boutique
http://www.amelli.co.il/

MONALINA Kids Clothing Boutique
http://www.monalina.com/

Yarin's Boutique
https://www.facebook.com/yarins.boutique